W9-DDI-396

Monographs on communication
technology and utilization

5

Rural radio:
programme formats

Kiranmani A. Dikshit
Ian Boden
Clifford Donkor
Simeon Bonzon
Hernando Bernal Alarcon
Jaroslav Košťál
Glenn Powell

Published in 1979 by the United Nations
Educational, Scientific and Cultural Organization
7 Place de Fontenoy, 75700 Paris
Printed by Imprimerie des Presses Universitaires
de France, Vendôme

ISBN 92–3–101616–4

© Unesco 1979
Printed in France

between city, the producers, and the farmers through

Preface

In the more than fifty years of radio broadcasting, the
farm forum is perhaps the best known type of rural broadcasting. But today, the broadcasters who created the farm
forum no longer use this format, although it has been
adapted in a number of ways in many countries of the
developing world: India, Zambia, Thailand, Philippines
and Ghana, to name a few. Meanwhile, other formats
have been developed for specific purposes and audiences.

In Nepal, for instance, the production team used
dialogue at first as a means of introducing the junior farm
technicians to the farmers. Later on, the dialogue between
a fictitious 'old lady' and the farm technician became the
main feature of the programme for presenting pros and
cons, difficulties and advantages, new techniques versus
old superstitions. This format has shown the importance
of presenting technical information in terms of the social
and cultural milieu of the audience.

In Papua New Guinea, a country of difficult terrain
and isolated communities and where radio is often the
only source of news, the producers directed their informational programmes towards agricultural technicians
and farm managers, as well as the farmers themselves. A

locally composed popular song *What Did the Didiman Do?* explains the role of field technicians and attunes the audience to their activities in the community.

Ghana has continued with the radio farm forum begun in 1964. Over the years, experience has shown the need for strong field organization and constant contact between the radio producers and the forums through visits, trade fairs, mobile reports and inter-forum projects. While the growth of forums has been slowed down in recent years, the production team has been careful not to encourage more forums than they can service, and to stress that the communities themselves rather than the radio production team should take prime responsibility for the forum organization.

In the Philippines, a community station adopted the magazine format for a public service type programme aimed at a provincial audience. The programme is centred on a studio announcer who maintains continuity for mobile reports, taped interviews, studio discussions and phoned-in reports. In a progressive rural capital, this format has shown the increased effectiveness of linking news events and public service to technical agricultural information.

The Acción Cultural Popular in Colombia selected drama, in both serial form and short spots, to focus on changing old ways of thinking, to reinforce new ideas and concepts, and to pave the way for field workers with specific follow-up lessons on responsible parenthood. This method demonstrates that radio can successfully discuss sensitive issues and touch upon deep-rooted attitudes; but specific technical instruction is more effectively handled by field workers.

In Czechoslovakia, farm broadcasting is actively oriented to national goals: concentration of land resources, co-operative farming, new techniques and conservation of resources. The programme, an open-magazine format, is researched, scripted and produced entirely by women. Close liaison is maintained with research institutes, the Rural Academy, and farm machinery development agencies. This programme shows how key information resources are composed into a lively action-oriented report, using telex, portable tape-recorders and field reporters.

Finally, the Canadian Broadcasting Corporation, the originator of the farm forums, has also settled into a magazine format, starting with international and national news, specialized market prices, and then dealing with interviews on current farm affairs, coverages of farm fairs and special problems. It is interesting to note that this format was dictated by the audience's desire to have straight information, up-to-date news, and in-depth reports—without any long music interludes, dramas or talky sessions. Over the years, rural broadcasting has constantly had to be adapted to the tastes, available time and information expectations of an audience exposed to other sources of information, especially television.

This monograph, the fifth in the series on communication technology and utilization, focuses on these various methods of reaching the rural audience for farm techniques, organization, up-to-date information and general rural development. Almost all of these programme surveys were prepared by the radio producers themselves. This monograph is not intended as a scientific study nor as a techniques manual. No attempt has been made to conclude that any one method is right or wrong, good or bad. The success of any of the formats or techniques discussed will depend greatly on the objectives, the audience and the broadcaster himself. It is hoped that, reading through these pages, fellow broadcasters, students of radio, writers and agriculture field agents, can cull from the experience of other programmes around the world and adapt usable ideas within their own programmes.

The authors are responsible for the choice and the presentation of the facts contained in this book, and for the opinions expressed therein, which are not necessarily those of Unesco and do not commit the Organization.

Contents

Kiranmani A. Dikshit

The old lady and the farmers

We started this farm programme in 1966 with one tape-recorder and three people with no formal training in radio production. We were given fifteen minutes of air time to reach 12 million people in the highest mountains of the world.

The problem of communication in Nepal is as high as the mountains. Some 12 million people live mainly on a subsistence agriculture of the rectangular-shaped country of 90,000 square kilometres. Nature divides Nepal into four major zones. Situated between the Indian frontier and the foothills of the Siwalik, the Tarai is a strip of flat alluvial plains 200 metres above sea level. The northern part of the Tarai is covered with marshes and jungle and is densely populated. This is our rice bowl.

The Siwalik hills rise straight out of the Ganges plain. There are very few villages in this chain which rises up to 2,000 metres.

Abrupt and gigantic, the Himalayas tower majestically with dense primaeval forests at 4,000 metres. Here

The author, Kiranmani Dikshit, is chief of the Agricultural Information Section, Katmandu, Nepal.

are found luxuriant, impenetrable underwood and magnificent trees—especially the famous Himalayan cedar. Rivers have eroded the mountain sides and formed wide valleys where the Tibetans dwell.

For centuries these mountains have not only protected Nepal from invasion, but also isolated it from modernization. Trade paths link towns and villages, but most of these are too steep to be made into vehicular roads. Travel is mainly on foot. People carry heavy loads in baskets, supported by a band across the forehead or on yokes across their shoulders. The 400-odd cars that were in the Katmandu valley before 1951 had to be carried by porters across the mountains from India.

There are two basic cultural traditions in Nepal, the Indo-Hindu tradition from the Tarai plains and the Buddhist tradition from the Himalayas in what is now known as Tibet. In the Katmandu valley, one can find the oldest Buddhist stupa in the world, Swyambhunath, and one of the holiest Hindu shrines, Pasupatinath. But many of the people still believe in evil spirits, witchcraft and superstition. If a paddy field is infested with insects, the farmers smoke the fields at night and beat drums, hoping that the evil spirits will go away and the insects will die. In this situation, where farm practices are tied in with customs and traditions, the farm broadcaster has to be careful not to counter tradition too roughly and possibly alienate his audience. This is just one of the challenges of scientific farming.

Most of the people speak the official language, Nepali, though there are at least forty dialects as well.

Life for the ordinary people has changed little in the last thousand years. The traditional *halo* is still the basic tool for ploughing the land. The whole family is engaged in farming from morning to night, from childhood to old age. Farming is the basic way of life. Hence, agriculture is one of the priority programmes of the government.

Field organization

Under the Ministry of Agriculture, sixty-seven of the seventy-five districts of the country have an Agricultural Development Office (ADO) each with a team of Junior

Technical Assistants (JTA). There are also seven agricultural stations and sixty-nine experimental farms at the service of the district ADOs. The JTAs organized farmers' clubs in their districts. Some of these clubs received the first batch of 150 radio sets for organized listening groups. The Food and Agricultural Organization (FAO) subsequently donated another 200 radios and studio equipment. The Agricultural Information Section supported the project with printed booklets, posters and other audio-visual aids. All sections of the ministries (fisheries, agronomy, horticulture, botany, veterinary, research and so forth) fed their data through the Agricultural Information Section to the ADOs from where the JTAs imparted the information and techniques to the farmers. In turn, the JTAs fed back information through the ADOs to the ministry.

The radio station

There is only one radio station in Nepal. Established in 1951, it is owned and managed by the government through the Ministry of Communication. It started with a 5-Kilowatt medium-wave transmitter but now uses a 100-Kilowatt short-wave transmitter as well. Broadcasts are staggered from 06.00 to 09.30 hours; from 13.00 to 16.00 hours and from 17.30 to 23.00 hours on medium and short waves.

The station accepts both government and paid commercial advertisements, but our programme under the Ministry of Agriculture is not sponsored by any commercial revenue. The station has been most co-operative, allowing us to record in our own studios, offering us access to their tape library for music and sound effects, providing air time of fifteen minutes three times a week. Although our make-shift studios cannot always produce the sound quality of the radio studios, especially in the early days, our programmes have always been accepted. Now with improved equipment, the production is of comparable quality to that of the radio station.

The farm programme

The earliest form of agricultural broadcasting on Radio Nepal consisted of reading from technical books or agricultural bulletins from the ministry. From the end of an FAO seminar on agricultural broadcasting in New Delhi in 1962, it took all of four years to get a more comprehensive and effective farm programme on the air.

In 1966, the Agricultural Information Section was formed and given the mandate to start rural broadcasts. With a staff of four, none of whom had any training in radio production, we were to produce two programmes per week of twenty minutes each. We worked on two basic formats which were further developed over the years.

Format 1: agricultural advice, 5 minutes; drama, 10 minutes; agricultural news, 5 minutes.

Format 2: instructions on farm operations or techniques, 5–7 minutes; dialogue between the JTA and an old lady, 12–15 minutes.

At the beginning we used the studios at the radio station, but due to heavy production schedules, our recording time was very limited and often postponed. So we decided to make our own recording studio. We covered the walls with heavy curtains, erected a partition with a double-glass window in order to isolate a control room, and bought a tape-recorder from a local store.

The programme grew steadily in popularity and in 1968 it was aired three times a week.

Rationale of the format

The most popular part of the three programmes has always been the dialogue between the JTA and the old lady. But why an old lady? In many Asian countries, where the extended family system prevails, there is very little work for the 'grandma' of the family. She is the boss and orders daughters and daughters-in-law alike, and everyone else. This old lady with practically no work to do sits in her open yard or under a tree, stops all the passers-by to ask where they are going, where they are coming from or what they are doing. The village is not big and therefore she usually knows everyone and what they are doing.

One day, someone told her that there was a new person in the village. 'He tells people how to do farming; he gives insecticides and *medicines*.' She was attracted by the word *medicine*, as she was suffering from gout and no one in the village could cure her. She thought maybe this JTA could help her with some of his *medicines*.

One evening she stopped the JTA on his way home from a field visit and as her usual inquisitive self got the better of her, she asked him about his work and (after many questions) where he might be able to get some medicine for her gout. He told her he was not a medicine man, but would try to get some medicine for her anyway the next time he came around. He was of course very polite, so as not to offend her.

After several days, the JTA returned and found the old lady sitting under a tree waiting for him. He knows what she will ask him and humbly offers his excuses, 'I'm sorry, grandma, I will definitely bring it next time.'

The purpose of using the old lady in the first few programmes was merely to introduce the 'newcomer', the JTA, to the village, and explain through his dialogue with the old lady what his purpose was—to offer advice, to counsel on farm techniques, to introduce insecticides and so forth. But as the old lady gained an unexpected popularity, we further developed her as an integral part of the format. Over the years, the old lady took an interest in the newcomer. She developed a small kitchen garden, then a paddy field, and then a few head of cattle. She naturally had many problems and so she kept a continuing dialogue with the JTA on when to harvest, how large to dig a fishpond (to be dug by her sons-in-law of course), where to find young fish, what are the farm operations for the next two to three weeks.

As a matter of fact, we could say almost all major farm information over the various seasons was transmitted through this dialogue between the JTA and the old lady, and in a very convincing way. The dialogue is spoken in the same manner in which the people in the village would hold their conversations. The JTA is tired and wants to go home, but the old lady drags it on until she is fully convinced. One government official told me: 'I am not that interested in the content of your old lady's programmes, but I like very much the way she speaks, presents her problems and detains the JTA only long enough to keep the audience interested, as any clever broadcaster would.'

On one of my rounds, I once met a farmer about ninety kilometres away from Katmandu on the way to Pokhra. With me was the production team, including the young girl who plays the part of the 'old lady'. The farmer was about 80 years old and had a family of twenty including grandchildren. He had four acres of land, a fruit orchard, ten head of improved swine, and a flock of 100 local and improved breeds of poultry. He also grew wheat, two crops of rice and pineapples. He was extremely proud to show us around his farm.

'I see you do know of the Junior Technical Assistant and the services of the Agricultural Development Office.'

'Yes, but he seldom comes here,' replied the farmer.

'Then, who advises you on all these farm operations, the piggery and the poultry?'

'That old lady, of course.'

'Which old lady? Can I meet her?'

'The old lady on the radio,' he said bursting into laugher. 'She is so cunning and very smart.'

'You mean you do all these farm operations, piggery and poultry merely by listening to that old lady's programme?'

'I never miss it because I get a lot of information out of it and I follow all I get. You see, we live so far from the town and the technicians visit us very seldom, so why should I go to anyone else when I can get all the information right in my own house? A few years back I was in trouble. I had to feed twenty hungry mouths and the produce was not enough. But since I started listening to that programme and followed the instructions, everything started getting better. Now I can save 10 to 20 rupees a year, deducting all my expenses and even the school fees for my grandsons. Oh, that old lady is good.'

'Why is she good? Because she speaks well?' I asked.

'No, no, she interrogates that JTA who tries to wind up too fast. This lady won't let him go until she is satisfied. This is what I like. It gives me an opportunity to get more information and the repetition makes it all very clear to us.'

Finally, I asked, a bit fearful of breaking credibility, 'Would you like to meet this old lady?'

'Who wouldn't? But I can't go to Katmandu, it costs money.'

'Well, suppose I bring her up here?'

'Please, sir, do not kid us.'

I introduced myself as the producer of the programme and explained that the young lady with me was the same 'old lady' of the programme, and that we were all part of the Agricultural Information Section doing support work for the field.

'But I can't believe it!'

'Yes, she is the one,' he exclaimed. And he called his wife and chidren and neighbours. It was a big occasion for the whole village.

The format today

With additional equipment, the format has become more flexible. We now have two mono tape-recorders for dubbing, mixing and editing; one four-track tape-recorder for playback; one four-channel mixer; and three cassette recorders for field recording and interviews. The programme is now aired four times a week for fifteen minutes at 18.45 hours.

The Sunday evening programmes are broken down as follows: opening, 45 seconds; spot, 3 minutes; interviews, 11.5 minutes; closing, 45 seconds—giving a total air time of 15 minutes. The brief spot touches on a farm activity coming up within a few days, such as spraying, new crops, or cattle-disease prevention. This is then followed by edited interviews with farmers, agricultural experts, researchers, co-operatives' agents, bank officers and the like.

The Monday evening programmes differ from the Sunday programmes in that the 11.5 minutes allowed for interviews is given over to the 'JTA-and-old-lady' dialogue. Over the years, the old-lady format has changed considerably. Previously concerned with the what and how of farming, this programme now focuses on the why of farming practices. The fifteen-minute segment is broadcast within the one-hour rural programme of Radio Nepal.

Programme support

The programme is conceived, scripted and produced entirely by the Radio Production Unit of the Agricultural Information Section. Linked to our radio work is the annual production of more than ninety booklets, leaflets and pamphlets and some thirty posters on various agricultural subjects. The radio team also assists in occasional farm exhibits and festivals thus providing radio support for these activities as well as information and report materials for the programme.

While the JTAs are not administratively linked to us, a number of them co-operate in the formation of listener clubs. The availability of more transistor radios and provision for training seminars could help in integrating the JTAs more into the radio work.

Feedback and evaluation

Regular information from the field comes from three main sources: letters from the radio audience; reports from JTAs who have organized listening clubs; and discussion with JTAs, field workers and agricultural officers during regular training seminars and workshops organized by the Agricultural Information Section.

The only major research touching on the programme was the 1974 survey on radio listening patterns in Nepal conducted by the New Educational Reform Associates.

The main conclusions of this survey, based on a random sample of fourteen of Nepal's seventy-five districts, are:

After the news programme, the agricultural programme is the most popular.

The agricultural programme has a regular audience of more than one-half of all radio owners; and occasionally covers 90 per cent of the audience.

By far the most popular format is the 'JTA and the old lady'.

The favourite listening time of the estimated 115,000 radio homes (now probably more than 200,000) is 07.00–08.00 hours and 19.00–20.00 hours, though now the commercial service is quickly gaining an audience in the 21.00–22.00-hour slot.

About two-thirds of the audience have incorporated one or more farm practices discussed on the programme. Those who did not, failed to do so because of lack of farm implements or money.

The survey concludes:

More generally, what all of our data imply is that radio is taken as a serious communications device by those who possess receivers as well as by those who do not. The two most popular radio programmes, news and agriculture, are basically informational, not entertainment; the second of these is blatantly educational. In addition, radio listening appears to be a deliberate, serious, regularized pattern in the daily activity of the owners and, to a lesser extent, of non-owners. Radio listening is not a haphazard affair in Nepal. For the listeners, it seems to fulfil a desire for an awareness of the things beyond the village. As such, it may be that radio's potential as an educational and motivational tool for national integration and development has only been very partially developed or utilized to date.

Other than this empirical survey, one need only consider the vast agricultural changes that have taken place in this country in the last ten years. A decade ago hardly any crops were grown after the paddy season. Today the whole country grows improved varieties of wheat. Before, only those in and around Katmandu could enjoy vegetables. Today people in the Tarai foothills also grow vegetables.

Even our approach in the radio programme has gradually changed from general farm practices to detailed instructions and more explanatory types of discussion.

It is extremely difficult, and even hazardous, to say that radio was a prime cause of any of these changes. There are several other development factors: the field workers, the agricultural printed information, increase of roads, marketing changes, and so forth. But certainly radio plays an important role in the cumulative impact of development forces. The data in Table 1 bring this out.

TABLE 1. *Percentage of radio owners and non-owners who obtain agricultural information from specified sources*

Source	Percentage of radio owners (N=266)	Percentage of non-owners (N=131)
JTA (extension agent)	50.4	40.5
Radio	41	16
Friends and other farmers	20.3	35.1
District agriculture and development office	6.4	8.4
Pamphlets	1.5	3.8
Research farms	0.4	2.3

Note: percentages do not total 100 because some of the respondents cited more than one source of agricultural information.

Conclusion

While the programme has progressed rapidly since its beginning almost a decade ago, there are a number of activities which, if seriously tackled, could serve to expand the range and efficiency of the programme.

Training. At present, only two people are actively engaged in the production of the programme. If expansion takes place, there will be need of more trained rural broadcasters. But there is no facility for training in rural broadcasting in Nepal.

Broadcasting language. All programmes are broadcast in Nepali, the national language, in an effort to strengthen national and cultural unity. However, this policy seems to reduce the audience in the Tarai, Siwalik and Midland regions. Consideration should be given to the possibility of special language programmes for these regions.

Evaluation. There is need of a central evaluation unit, probably under the auspices of Radio Nepal, which would review programmes originated by Radio Nepal and user ministries and offices, and make concrete practical suggestions to gear programmes more closely to development goals.

Expansion of listening clubs. There are at present about 150 listening clubs. Because of the high cost of radios, owners are likely to be limited to the wealthier classes. There should be some means of importing low-cost radios, lowering tariffs, or some sort of government subsidy in order to allow more widespread availability of radios to more people.

Extract of script between the JTA and the old lady: 'compost manure'

OLD LADY: Oh, the JTA has not turned up till now, what could have happened?

JTA: I've been here all the time.

OLD LADY: Why did you come from the back, son? I didn't see you coming.

JTA: The road is at your back, I couldn't possibly come from the front, could I? And you don't expect me to walk through the field do you, grandma?

OLD LADY: No, no, son, you should not do that, you must walk on the main road.

JTA: That's right, and that's why I came from the main road.

OLD LADY: You seem to be in a very happy mood today, but, son, I am very cross with you.

JTA: [laughing] Look, look, grandma . . .

OLD LADY: No, no, no, I am really angry with you, ah, what should I say—you seem to be getting old.

JTA: [muttering to himself] Yes, every day I am getting older by one day.

OLD LADY: You asked me to put that sugar-like [ammonium sulphate] manure in my wheat, and I did [cough]. When I visited the field after a few days, you know, I found all the leaves curled and twisted. I was shocked to see it. Then I thought of watering it a little. Why did you tell me to do it like that?

JTA: Now look, grandma, don't you remember? I told you to irrigate after spreading the fertilizer on the plot.

OLD LADY: All this happened and now where do I stand? You know all the villagers envy me because I met you and farm as you advise and I am prospering.

JTA: Didn't I ask you then if you understood, grandma. And nicely you said 'Yes I did' but now I am getting all the blame. How should I know you did not understand?

OLD LADY: But I did what you told me to do, son.

JTA: You did not do as I said, except to apply the fertilizer. Didn't I tell you to irrigate it after applying the fertilizer? You must irrigate it, grandma, but, thank God, at least you gave a little water or all would have died.

OLD LADY: What should I do? I was hoping 'now I'll get a good crop', but . . .

JTA: Look here, grandma, if you are cooking rice without water, will it cook? No it won't, you must put water in it, right?

OLD LADY: Yes, son, we must put water in it.

JTA: Similarly, unless we irrigate, the chemical does not dissolve and the plants cannot absorb it and the chemical is wasted.

OLD LADY: Then I irrigated it late, son.

JTA: Yes, you should have irrigated immediately after applying the fertilizer and . . . why did it curl up? . . . You must have put more on than I told you.

OLD LADY: Maybe, son, then how much should I put?

JTA: You should never apply more than the recommended amount.

OLD LADY: Is that so, son?

JTA: Yes, grandma. Different crops can take only a certain amount and . . . from now on never say 'I understand, son' when you are not clear, I will gladly tell you twice, thrice or more.

OLD LADY: Right, son, I will remember this, but what had happened to me then was that I thought I understood it clearly.

JTA: Maybe at that time, though you were listening to me, you were thinking of something else. Maybe you were worrying 'how can I go on this pilgrimage?'.

OLD LADY: No, son, I am not thinking about going on this pilgrimage, but I have other worries to worry about, see I am old now.

JTA: [laughing] Oh, why, you have sons and grandsons. They will take care of everything, why do you worry?

OLD LADY: Yes they will, then why I am running here and running there at this age? Now, son, what are you going to tell me today?

JTA: Today I . . . well . . . as we were discussing the fertilizer, why don't I tell you about the compost manure?

OLD LADY: Oh I know about this manure, don't you make it in a pit and then you can add as much as you can in the field and the field does not go bad?

JTA: Yes, you are right, it is made in the pit and you can apply as much as you want.

OLD LADY: How come?

JTA: Because there are good things in it that make this manure better than the chemical manure.

OLD LADY: I know only that by adding this in the field I get little more yield. That's all.

JTA: You see, by adding this in the field it not only adds nitrogen but it adds humus and makes the field fertile, you might have heard someone say that by using commercial fertilizers the fields are getting spoiled.

OLD LADY: You are right, son, even my own field is spoiled.

JTA: That's not true, it's you who are spoiling the field, you remember I told you that certain fertilizers help vegetative growth, and others help plants grow bigger pods, strong stock and this protects or makes the plant resistant to disease. But where is that thing which makes the soil fertile or improves the soil structure or texture?

OLD LADY: Yes, go on.

JTA: So you require something to add which will improve the soil structure and texture, so something should be added, don't you think?

OLD LADY: Yes, something must be added.

JTA: And that thing you can get from this compost which is made in the pit, and it also contains other minerals required for the plants. Its main function is to improve soil condition, as for example . . .

OLD LADY: By this compost manure, son?

JTA: Yes, if you have some loam soil . . .

OLD LADY: Yes, yes.

JTA: And if it is sandy, it loosens the soil and increases the water-holding capacity and adds humus. You can get many crops.

OLD LADY: Oh!

JTA: So these are the advantages of this manure over the chemical fertilizers.

OLD LADY: Yes, son.

JTA: There is one thing, you should be very careful, don't put raw cow dung without letting it decompose, remember last year you said that all your egg plant was destroyed by some grub?

OLD LADY: Yes, yes.

JTA: And all blame came on me for giving you those seedlings?

OLD LADY: Yes, my son, yes, I remember.

JTA: But it wasn't my fault, and I remember I showed you the grub which destroyed the seedlings. . . .

OLD LADY: You know I am not cross with you always, but I like you very much.

JTA: When I showed you the cut worm you were surprised to see that that little grub could destroy such a lot. Now when you put raw cow dung on the land, the grubworms like it for laying eggs.

OLD LADY: That's where those grubs come from.

JTA: If you decompose the cow dung, the eggs are killed, you can also add wasted weeds and other materials and you get manure and good crops. But you must also add lime. . . .

OLD LADY: Yes, son, sometimes we can get lime in the village.

JTA: When it is available in the market, buy some and store it. Then you can add a little while making compost. By adding lime the soil does not get alkaline. Sometimes you might have seen yellow patches on the crops. This is often caused by the alkalinity in the soil.

OLD LADY: So you have to add lime, son.

JTA: If you add lime, that will not happen.

OLD LADY: Is that so, son?

JTA: You see, the field also needs lime, water and fertilizer to give you good crops—and there are sixteen other minerals . . . of course I will have to explain to you in detail later. You won't understand now.

OLD LADY: Yes, I won't understand unless you explain.

JTA: But definitely there are advantages to adding lime to the soil.

OLD LADY: I will get some, son, it's not a big thing. Moreover, I have bought more expensive things for my needs.

JTA: Yes, now you must add this compost very frequently to the field, it is just like cooking food without salt. You may add all chemical fertilizers but without compost it is not complete. Tell me how food tastes without salt?

OLD LADY: It doesn't taste good.

Ian Boden

The farmers' session

Rural programmes have changed a lot since they were started more than fifteen years ago. There is today a keener sense of knowing the audience—be it urban or rural, be they farmers or agricultural technicians. There is also a greater movement to national unity, while at the same time a constant recognition of the need to be relevant to each region and province.

On the several islands that comprise the newly independent State of Papua New Guinea, vast changes are constantly challenging rural radio, both providing a solid infrastructure for communication and setting new targets to achieve. While the government has set national goals in its Eight-point Development Plan, the emphasis has been on strengthening provincial leadership in the several sectors. Since independence, there has been an upswing in the devolution of power and authority to officers at the local level. This has brought about a rapid increase in the number of provincial governments, which is expected to stabilize in nineteen or twenty local assemblies by 1981.

The author, Ian Boden, is a training officer with the National Broadcasting Commission, Port Moresby, Papua New Guinea.

The government resettlement scheme has effected the redistribution of land from overseas plantation owners to individual owner-farmers who till the soil for both subsistence and cash crops. The rise of this new class of rural landowner has created a new set of information needs.

The 1977 National Broadcasting Development Plan stresses the development of provincial radio stations and intercommunication between the provinces and the capital. At the completion of the plan in 1982–83, three programme services will be reaching the people via several medium-wave and short-wave network systems. The seventeen provincial radio stations, already in operation, will be transmitting on new, higher powered medium-wave transmitters; trained staff will be producing programmes from additional studios. Complementing the Kalang (national) and Kundu (provincial) programme services, a third service, Karai, will stress rural development, education and national issues. A special feature of this service is that many of the programmes will originate from the provincial stations and be carried over the national network.

It is against this background of independence and the provincial structure of government, leadership, and development, that rural broadcasting in Papua New Guinea must be viewed.

Setting

Papua New Guinea is a group of islands just below the Equator, east of Indonesia, north of Australia. Its 2.8 million people inhabit 461,000 square kilometres of an extremely varied land mass: mangrove swamps that gird the coasts for hundreds of kilometres; inland swamps whose annual floods create lakes as deep as four metres; dense groves of sago palm; rolling savannah grasslands; rain forests covering three-quarters of the country; and the more than 1,500-metre-high Mount Wilhelm.

Despite road-building efforts, land travel is difficult. Contact with some villages takes two to three weeks on foot through the forests or by canoe along the coast. Whether overland or between the islands, air travel is faster and surer. At the provincial level there is more interpersonal contact among the rural folk themselves.

Despite the variety of terrain, actually only 1 per cent is suitable for commercial agriculture; another 24 per cent is used for various kinds of non-commercial farming; 4 per cent for grazing; the remaining 71 per cent is unfit for any kind of profitable agricultural development.

Even with these limited land resources, the economy is still based on primary production: coconuts and coconut products, high-grade coffee, cocoa, quality tea, palm oil, timber, rubber. Alternate cash crops are being encouraged in order to diversify production and reduce the country's vulnerability to price fluctuations on the international market. These crops include pepper, pyrethrum, passion fruit, peanuts, cardomom and other spices.

The sea on the other hand provides a rich paradise not only in food resources (barracuda, crayfish, prawn, tuna, *bêche-de-mer*) but also for cultured pearls, especially in the southern part of the country. Lakes and rivers teem with trout and carp. To further tap these natural riches, a Fisheries College was recently established in Kavieng on the northern island province of New Ireland. With the expected announcement of a national 200-mile fishing limit in common with other South Pacific maritime countries, sea-based industries will be playing an increasingly more important economic role in the future.

Papua New Guinea embraces more than 700 separate languages but no more than six have wide usage. Increasingly, Neo-Melanesian (a language with English, German, and vernacular words) is becoming the lingua franca of the country though, in remote rural areas, the local vernaculars are the only way to communicate. Despite the variety of languages and customs, there are signs of an awakening Melanesian identity, particularly among the more exposed members of the community. The country is on the whole nominally Christian—another unifying element.

Because of the geographical complexity of the country, the isolating terrain, the slowness of postal service and other communications, radio broadcasts become an important instant-information source for all sectors of society—the rural masses, community leaders, provincial and national officers. And it is vital that radio help form the needed social links both in the individual communities and in the nation as a whole.

Audience

Although the programme seeks to reach all kinds of people engaged in agricultural activities, the main target audience can be divided into two main groups: the urban-based agronomist and the rural-based land holders. Trying to cultivate both groups with the variety of languages and farm problems is in itself a major task.

The more challenging group, however, is that of the rising self-employed farm owner. He possesses a small plot of land which he works for cash crops, particularly cocoa, copra and palm oil. Some may have a secondary education, though by far the majority have completed only primary school. This means that most have only a rudimentary grasp of English. Those who have had less exposure to the world outside their community tend to maintain an insular outlook, slow to accept new techniques or marketing concepts. This is particularly true in the coffee-growing areas of the highlands where many have not even travelled outside their own province.

These listeners will be especially interested in current prices for the crops they grow, new techniques likely to increase productivity in their area, special agricultural demonstrations, news of agricultural shows and exhibitions—particularly those in which the farmers can participate. When communicating with this sector of the audience, the broadcaster must try to emphasize local and provincial activities in order to gain their interest. On the other hand, he must also try to break down the resistance to ideas from the outside. When using a local language to win over a particular locality, he must be careful not to alienate other listeners who do not understand that language. In all cases, complex ideas and techniques must be explained in the simplest, most basic terms.

Urban listeners offer another set of challenges to the rural broadcaster. These are professional agronomists, development officers of various government departments, managers of commercial farms or agricultural companies. The urban listener is usually young, well educated (a university degree from an agricultural or administrative school), and lives in Port Moresby or one of the larger provincial capitals.

His specialization may be agricultural planning, farm management, technical development assistance or other liaison work between the farmers or farm industries and the banks or marketing groups. Even though he forms a numerical minority of the total audience, he plays an important role in the plans, decisions and management of the total agro-industrial sector. As a sophisticated listener, he expects a sophisticated format—straight information, up-to-date news, the latest in techniques and developments on the agricultural front. He must have information on farming and agriculture from other parts of the world, but he expects this information to be related to the particular local situations in the country. Information without relevance is of little use. As a key information source himself, he in turn expects radio to keep him well informed. This is all the more true for those development officers and farm managers in the outlying provinces who only with difficulty have access to other sources of information. For many of the provincial-based government development officers, radio is their only contact with the policies, plans and developments at the head office.

Radio

Radio broadcasting was introduced in Papua New Guinea in 1934 by the Amalgamated Wireless of Australia (AWA), but was discontinued in 1939 for security reasons during the Second World War. Broadcasting was reintroduced in 1944 with the assistance of the Australian Broadcasting Commission (ABC) and the Allied Forces.

Two years later, ABC took over full responsibility, but mainly to provide a programme service for expatriates. By 1961, radio stations had been established in fifteen provinces.

Soon after independence, the National Broadcasting

Commission (NBC) was created by an Act of Parliament in December 1973. The content and standards of broadcasting are directly controlled by the commission headed by a chairman/general manager, whose tenure is renewable every three years. The political integrity and independence of the commission is assured by the Broadcasting Act and NBC's own constitution.

In May 1977, a development plan was finalized. This plan stressed the improved technical facilities using higher powered medium- and short-wave transmitters, additional production studios, and the strengthening of provincial radio.

To do this, the plan proposed the organization of three programme networks: (a) the Kalang Service, broadcasting to the entire nation in English over a network of medium- and short-wave transmitters; (b) the Kundu Service, a network of seventeen provincial radio stations originating their own material over the new medium-wave transmitters to be commissioned during the development period; (c) the Karai Service, which will be developed to stress developmental and educational programmes. A key feature of the Karai Service will be the origination of an increasingly larger number of programmes from various provincial stations to be relayed over the other two networks (see Figure 1 for a schema of proposed network services and transmission networks).

In May 1977, a commercial service was introduced but within a framework of guidelines that avoids the direct

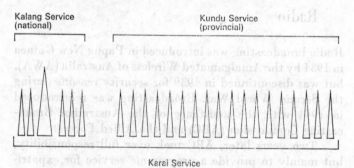

FIG. 1. Programmes originate at one or several of the Kundu stations and are relayed over the national or Kalang network.

sponsoring of individual programmes. This provides an additional source of revenue for broadcasting supported mainly by government funds.

The production unit

Under NBC, the Rural Broadcast Department is responsible for all programmes dealing with agriculture and primary industry, both at the national and the provincial levels. The department is headed by the supervisor of rural broadcasts, who assures the co-ordination and development of programmes and is responsible for maintaining high standards of quality. The assistant supervisor oversees production, draws up the rosters and manages the daily operations. The four senior rural broadcast officers handle research, scripting, editing and presentation of the programmes.

Each of the provincial stations also has a rural broadcast officer, who is in charge of producing a wide range of agricultural and extension programmes aimed specifically at subsistence and cash-crop farmers in their regions. Some of these materials are also sent to the head office for inclusion in the national rural programme. The head office in turn dispatches material of special interest to certain provinces for airing on the local stations. This assures a constant flow of programme material to and from the provinces.

At both the national and provincial levels, close liaison is maintained with the development officers of the Department of Primary Industry. Many of these officers contribute significantly to the various rural programmes and are encouraged to participate in broadcasting courses sponsored by NBC.

The Rural Broadcasts Department, like all the programme departments of NBC, has its own dubbing and editing facilities. In addition the department also possesses portable tape-recorders and some cassette recorders. Cassettes are seldom used because the sound quality is generally below that required for broadcasting. For production of programmes, the department has access to the main studios at NBC, which are completely equipped with a multi-input console, capable of mixing four turntables, four tape-recorders and several microphones. When needed, cartridge recorders are also available. Dubbing programmes for the provincial stations can be done in the adjacent studio which has a multi-dub rack of recorders.

The Transcription and Tape Library stocks more than 40,000 records and a number of taped rural programmes from other countries. The Reference Library offers up-to-date books, journals and publications on rural topics. The Tape Archives Library countains many of the rural programmes since their beginning in Papua New Guinea.

For field assignments, NBC has a fleet of vehicles at the disposal of the Rural Broadcasts Department, but usually the vehicles are selected for their ability to negotiate the difficult terrain to be covered by our fieldmen. These trips are usually planned around special programmes covering provincial agricultural shows, or gathering material for a series on coffee-growing developments or progress in the palm-oil industry. To economize on travel and enhance local rapport, many of these field assignments are given to the provincial rural broadcast officer, who in turn supplies the head office with fresh local information.

As mentioned in a previous section, rough terrain also requires the rural broadcaster to trek into the field or paddle along the coasts to reach isolated areas. For this work, in areas without electricity, it is imperative to have sturdy recording equipment and sure battery power.

To assure a highly competent rural-broadcasts team, the current minimum requirement is that candidates have a recognized certificate from an agricultural college, at least two years' rural field experience, including agricultural extension work, and some knowledge of rural broadcasting techniques. In order to maintain quality programmes on the air, the Division of Staff Development and Training holds regular workshops of two weeks' duration on documentaries, discussion programmes and interviewing techniques. For special courses on rural broadcasting, agricultural officers from the Department of Primary Industry are also invited to help relate rural broadcast programmes to the needs of specific rural areas.

Such courses are also held at the provincial stations with several of the development officers from the DPI both assisting and participating.

The training complex in Port Moresby comprises a hostel for the participants, two seminar rooms and a suite of two studios. One studio is large enough to hold twenty-five trainees. The other is a replica of a typical studio in a provincial station, so that trainees can learn in a setting that is immediately translatable to their situation back home. The two seminar rooms are equipped with slide projectors, video equipment, and tape-playback facilities.

The programme

The programme today is more than fifteen years old, having its origins in an earlier rural programme designed when the Australian Broadcasting Commission was managing radio in Papua New Guinea. At that time the programme was called *Countryman's Session* and its content, format and presentation were slanted towards the expatriate plantation manager or agricultural technician. Large segments of the programme were composed of taped material from Australia with interviews, crop reports and information on new technology. While the programme served its stated aim, it was incomprehensible to most of the local population.

Although broadcasters of Papua New Guinea were involved in the programme almost from the start, their role was limited.

As Papua New Guineans became more involved in the agricultural sector and the colleges turned out more agricultural graduates towards the early 1960s, the programme took on a stronger orientation towards the local rural communities. The title was changed to *Farmers' Session* and the schedule of the programme was changed from 12.30 hours, after the noon news (when most expatriates came home for lunch), to 21.06 hours after the evening news when the Papua New Guineans were home and relaxed.

By 1970, three years before independence and the

creation of the National Broadcasting Commission, the staff, format, content and presentation were almost entirely nationalized.

The programme is aired Monday to Friday from 21.06 to 21.30 hours. On Saturdays, a fifteen-minute programme for home gardeners is featured from 08.00 to 08.15 hours; Sunday is for discussion of current events from 16.00 to 16.30 hours.

Farmers' Session is opened with a theme played by a local string band and has now become a familiar identification signature tune. The main format of the programme is information, discussion, interview and summary, bridged with short music pieces.

In selecting music, care is taken to assure that it is appropriate to the themes being discussed, representative of the various regions and, when possible, directly associated with farms and farm life. Some jingles have been recorded by local artists. One in particular, *What Did the Didiman Do?* even became a hit record and was requested on the *Listeners' Choice* music programme. This was especially beneficial for both agricultural development and rural broadcast officers, as *didiman* is the Neo-Melanesian word for agricultural extension officer.

There are also certain occasions when it becomes useful and even necessary to apply drama forms to rural programmes. This is especially so when trying to avoid lengthy explanation or when seeking to overcome opposition to new practices or new technology. In these and other cases, a short five- to six-minute drama drives home the point clearly and within a real-life situation.

Discussion among several people (technicians, local officers, farmers) as opposed to monologue is another effective method of conveying information and different points of view. Discussion usually sparks interest and attracts those who would usually not tune in to the farm programme. It also stirs controversy and polarizes viewpoints.

To build up listenership, *Farmers' Session* makes use of a number of thirty-second and one-minute promotional spots during other time-slots of the day. In addition, the programme receives mention in articles in the *Post Courier* (an English daily newspaper) and the national weekly

Neo-Melanesian newspaper, *Wantok*, plus publicity support from various leaflets and brochures circulated by the Office of Information and the Department of Primary Industry. With the assistance of the NBC staff, the Department of Primary Industry has issued *Rural Broadcaster Handbook No. 2* which provides rural extension officers with information on radio equipment and techniques.

Evaluation

Unfortunately there has not been any formal evaluation of the rural programmes. On general information, however, the Bureau of Statistics undertook a random national survey of villages and discovered that of more than 9,000 villages in the country, each had at least one functioning radio set; on the average there were five radio sets per village. The survey also pointed out that by far the largest group of regular listeners was under 30 years of age, and more likely to tune in to English programmes.

Balancing any lack of evaluative research, it can be said that there has always been a close working relationship between the development and extension officers of the Department of Primary Industry and the Rural Broadcast Officers, both at national and provincial levels. This has led to co-ordinated efforts in agricultural development campaigns, resettlement projects and an educational project to disseminate information on economic co-operatives. In the case of the latter, although the course was meant primarily for rural co-operative managers attending the course in the college, radio, through its interviews, taped summaries and other news programmes, was able to provide the same information for many other listeners whose interest would otherwise be marginal.

Inasmuch as the programme regularly features a comprehensive range of information, farm news, relevant simple technology, product prices, and agricultural personalities in a varied format aimed at both the village and urban listeners, it can be said that the programme is achieving its aims. More specific feedback information on effects, reception and changes brought about through the programme would help in formulating more definitive strategies and techniques.

There is one aspect of the programme that will become increasingly more important and that is the role radio will play in breaking down rural insularity. As with any new nation seeking national identity, there are long-held traditions associated with land usage and marketing, customs and patterns of life that eventually must change with the advance of modernity. In this regard, it is felt that Papua New Guinea's system of national, provincial, and the new Karai (development-oriented programme service) will be a conducive force in forging national unity while at the same time giving meaning and importance to the local communities. This balance of programme sources (national and local) is intended to overcome the inherent dangers of an over-centralized one-way, narrow-minded broadcasting system.

Clifford Donkor

The rural-radio forum

*It takes a lot of dedication to be a rural broadcaster, especially to
service rural radio forums. There is very little incentive to drive
your Land Rover for hours, park and walk for kilometres through
forests and rivers to find the forum villages. And yet field visits
are the key to successful forums. These provide the broadcaster
important feedback information, a grasp of the situation, and
make the farmers a more integral part of the entire forum
organization.*

The radio farm forum started in Ghana more than fourteen
years ago, but the idea started in Canada as early as 1940
and was tried out in India in 1954. Similar radio forums
have also been organized in Nepal, Thailand and Zambia.
Today the farm forum is no longer a new idea, but,
adequately organized, it can lead to solving many community problems: make farm technical information more
available; promote a sense of cohesion and co-operation in
rural communities; spur leadership and shared decision-
making; provide a means of contact between the villages
and national development programmes.

The author, Clifford Donkor, is a rural programmes producer with the Ghana
Broadcasting Corporation, Accra, Ghana.

This article explains the origins and establishment of radio farm forums in Ghana, shows how they are operating today, and provides some observations on the radio forum concept and how it can be applied more effectively to development objectives.

Ghana's 10 million people inhabit 238,000 square kilometres wedged between the Ivory Coast and Togo. For convenience, we can divide the country into four major geographical zones: the coast on the south; the dense forests occupying one-third of the entire territory in the south-west corner; the Volta Lake region formed at the delta of the Volta River; and the savannah in the north, at the rim of the Sahelian country of Upper Volta.

The principal occupation is agriculture (cocoa, corn and vegetable farming), but the country is also rich in minerals, especially gold, bauxite, manganese and diamonds. There is abundant fishing in the lake region and along the coast. But despite the volume of corporate mining and agriculture (Ghana is the source of a quarter of the world's cocoa exports), the basic way of life is farming, and in many cases subsistence farming. While agricultural volume may be high, actual productivity per hectare is below average: hence the need for improved farming techniques and use of media to reach the farmers.

All broadcasting in the country is carried out entirely by the Ghana Broadcasting Corporation (GBC), whose operations are supported by government subsidies, subscriptions and advertising revenue.

GBC broadcasts on short wave and VHF-FM from three transmission points, Accra, Ejura and Tema. Languages used on the home service are Akan, Ewe, Dagbani, Ga, Hausa, Nzema and English: the external service broadcasts in English, French, Swahili, Arabic, Portuguese and Hausa. GBC has its own training school for both radio and television. Diploma and degree courses are also available at the School of Journalism and Communication Studies, University of Ghana (Legon), which now has a basic radio and television studio for training. But there is no facility for training specifically in rural broadcasting.

Background

Rural broadcasting in Ghana began in 1962 with an invitation from the Australian Broadcasting Commission to send a rural technician from Ghana to study rural broadcasting in Australia. This was followed over the years by other training fellowships and courses in Canada, Federal Republic of Germany, Kenya and other countries, as well as Australia. In 1963, GBC started rural broadcasting with a weekly programme in Akan, the language spoken by about 60 per cent of the people. The following year, a daily thirty-minute programme for women was started. And late in 1964 the radio farm-forum project was initiated under the responsibility of GBC with the technical and financial assistance of Unesco and the External Aid Office of the Government of Canada, in response to a recommendation made by the Moshi meeting of Educational Broadcasters in Africa in 1962.

Even with the early modest beginnings in rural broadcasting, it was obvious that rural programmes alone would not solve basic problems of organization, adult education, complicated instructions in farming techniques and group co-operation at village level. Radio had to do more than broadcast; it had to reach out to the people. The organization of forums invited villagers to voice and discuss their own problems, encouraged participation in village affairs and co-operative activities, provided a means for identifying the villagers' interests in the decisions made by the forum. In addition, the forum provided an important social occasion for the village.

Sixty experimental forums and forty control forums were organized for the project in Akan-speaking communities. The United Farmers' Council Co-operatives released eight of their agricultural extension officers to train in rural broadcasting. GBC provided all studio and field equipment, training and personnel facilities, supported by international consultants.

After the forums were organized in the communities, the project undertook five major activities: (a) dissemination of visual aids and printed programme guides based on the theme of the coming broadcasts; (b) broadcast of the programmes; (c) organized group discussion; (d) organized group action; (e) feedback reports and evaluation.

For the project period, a list of topics was selected to include a wide range of activities relevant to rural communities.[1] The calendar of broadcasts, the printed guides, and a pre-broadcast questionnaire were sent to the villages before the first programme was aired. Posters were hung in key meeting points in the communities. After each programme, the secretary of the forum prepared a report on the broadcast and the activities taken up by the forum. After every third broadcast a special talk-back programme was arranged in which forum members were invited to the station to participate in a review/feedback discussion.

The programme today

Some fourteen years after the original project began, we are still continuing with the forums. After the first 100 forums were organized, the number grew to 200 in 1968 to over 300 in 1971, and today our target is 500. If the growth has been comparatively slow, it is because much of the support of the original project has been reduced and the excitement has died down. Moreover, owing to logistical constraints, we cannot organize more forums than we can handle.

There are now three weekly forum programmes broadcast in Akan, Ewe and Dagbani. These are broadcast in the evenings between 18.15 and 19.15 hours on Sundays, Mondays and Fridays. They are preceded by the local news and followed by a health programme.

The format consists of: signature tune; opening;

1. List of forum topics: prospects for farmers in the seven-year development plan; the principle of loans and state subsidies to farmers; distribution and marketing of crops and foodstuffs; the problem of storage of perishable crops; new trends in agriculture; foreign trade; family budgeting; career opportunities in rural areas; eat your way to good health; safeguards to national health; opportunities for the handicapped; education—the key to progress; the modern concept of the family; the influence of traditional institutions on educational development in Ghana; the role of religion in our changing society.

introduction of guests for the discussion; discussion; feedback mail and reports of forum activities; announcements of new forums to be inaugurated; and, finally, closing and signature.

The earlier forums were organized with the help of several score field and extension workers from various agricultural and social work offices. In general, field organizers went round the villages and with the help of the local chiefs and elders explained the objectives of the forum to the people. With the field organizer the people then set about electing officers (chairman and secretary) and prepared a place for group listening. While the chairman need not be an educated person, the secretary had to have at least basic writing skills in order to file the weekly reports to be sent to the station. A sample report is as follows:

RURAL RADIO FORUM REPORT

FORUM: Agbozume
SECRETARY: Kwaku Alipodjie Cudjoe
PLACE OF MEETING: Abganu Square
DISCUSSION LEADER: G. C. Ketorwoo
DISTRICT: Ketu
NUMBER PRESENT: 25
NUMBER ABSENT: 46
ADDRESS: P.O. Box 27, Agbozume

Report on broadcast

The problem of water in the villages

Water is becoming a critical problem in the villages. Yes, there are shallow wells, but in the dry season these dry up and it is difficult to find enough water to cook. There is piped water in the larger towns and some can carry it in margarine cans back to their villages. But often some people in the towns sell this piped water! And other people bringing the water in cans sell it in turn to the villages, making a wicked business of a vital necessity.

Beyond this there are also problems of diseased water—worms and bilharzia. Of course the villagers can boil the water, strain it to get the dirt and large objects out of it, put alum in it, but all this is very messy, time-consuming and fussy work for a household of ten people.

Some towns are fortunate in having deep wells and generator-fed pumps. But when there is a shortage of fuel or when conniving attendants charge excessive fees for pumped water, this aggravates the situation.

Ironically, we are near the River Volta, at the very delta, and yet water is a problem! We need a project that can utilize this gigantic source and provide water for everyone.

Therefore, we recommend:

1. All villages that can dig a well should do so, being careful to keep it clean and free of disease and worms.
2. The water-pump station at Agbozume should be supplied with two large generators to assure constant supply, as it is now serving many other towns (Klikor, Dzodze-Penyi, Abor, Akatsi).
3. Where possible, villages should be supplied with regular piped water.
4. The government should take up a massive study and project in order to tap the water of the Volta for the entire region. This project should be given top priority and delegated to a highly trustworthy body.

Organizing new forums

Over the years, however, we have worked on another approach, which seems to have led to the formation of more stable forums. We selected target areas on a relief map (to determine proximity to other villages, levels of development, possible local problems) and set up discussion programmes illustrating what forums could do in that area. We then explained how people in the area could contact the radio producer of the forum programmes or the field organizer in their area. Letters received from this motivational campaign were then read and discussed on the following programme, while the villagers were encouraged to organize, elect officers and have their first discussions. In case some had not heard the programme, the field organizer was instructed to visit the village with his portable recorder and run playbacks of the programme. After the villagers had organized and started some activities, and their reports were coming in regularly, we then prepared for a formal inauguration of the forum or forums, using either portable tape-recorders or the mobile recording van. Meanwhile, air time was allocated for continuously encouraging new activities of up-and-coming forums, and the organization of new forums in the target area. This, incidentally, was usually heard by other communities who were also prompted to organize their forums. Because these forums were strongly motivated beforehand and had already organized for action before the formal inauguration, they usually lasted longer and engaged in substantial activities. On average, inauguration did not take place until a year after the first contact with the community. To the inauguration we tried to invite special guests, government officials and members of the press, to make it a memorable occasion for the village.

Very often the village chief is an active member of the forum and often becomes the chief patron of its various activities, lending his personal and 'political' support.

Forum activities

All forums are always encouraged to undertake earning activities in order to purchase their own forum radio, to obtain secretarial supplies, etc. These are usually communal projects, such as vegetable gardening or animal breeding. As needed, forums are also spurred to collaborate in group or village activities, such as irrigation digging, preparing a festival, building village clinics, constructing feeder roads and marketing centres, testing out new seed varieties and farming methods.

One striking example of cohesion and initiative occurred in 1971 when the Settlement Farm sponsored by the Ghana Government and the Federal Republic of Germany at Agbate, near Peki Wudome, needed volunteers to help harvest an enormous bumper crop. Forums in the Peki-Djake (Volta Lake region) were called in to assist. They not only came but also suggested that the occasion be used to convoke a regional conference of rural forums. Officials from the Food and Agriculture Organization and GBC came to address the forums. Apart from the success of the conference, the bumper crop of corn was completely harvested.

Another collective effort was the response to the breakout of bilharzia (blindness caused by snails) in Todome, Peki. The field organizer in this area informed medical officials in Peki and the Ministry of Health about the epidemic. Peki forums joined in to bring pure water from the Ho region capital. Medical officers brought injections and medicine. These two incidents show that forums can be effective in stimulating group action and self-help.

The production unit

As with the original programme, the production unit today is part of GBC. Although there are some commercially sponsored programmes, the radio farm-forum programme is supported solely by GBC.

Under the rural programmes producer, there are two regional rural officers in the field, two other rural programme producers who prepare other farm programmes, one technician and one programme operator. All received their broadcasting training at GBC's training school. Though two have received some agricultural training, only the programme producer has studied rural science at the university level. Over the years, short training courses abroad have been made available to some of the production staff.

For the field, there are three portable tape-recorders and a mobile recording van on request.

Support for the programme

The earlier forums (during the project period) were given free radio sets. Today, we cannot afford to donate free radios and the people often have difficulty in finding financial sources to cover the cost of a simple radio. About half of the households in Ghana have radios, but the proportion diminishes as one travels north of the forest and lake regions. In the north, the availability of radio sets is a critical problem in the organization of viable forums. Outside of the broadcast itself, occasional field visits, and the presence of a handful of field organizers, there is no other form of financial or technical support for the forums. Even the calendar of programmes and discussion guides were stopped a few years ago due to financial restraints. The only print support we have now are the mimeographed forms for membership enrolment, a one-page paper on the duties of the chairman and secretary, and the feedback report. For forum inaugurations to which important guests or government officials have been invited, there may be a short item in the newspaper.

Feedback and evaluation

After the first formal research on the original radio forum project, there has been no other comprehensive study on the forums in Ghana. Our main source of information from the field has been the reports of the forums themselves or the written or oral reports of our own field organizers. Because of slow postal facilities, mail usually comes in a week late, but over a hundred reports are received regularly. To encourage more reports, those received are mentioned by name, their activities encouraged, their questions answered by farm specialists, and the field organizer is encouraged to visit villages sending in regular reports.

At times, active forums are invited to send a delegation to the station to participate in one of the discussion programmes. It is interesting to note that no written invitation is sent. They are cordially invited over the air and invariably a large number of the villagers do come.

Observations

Before coming to any conclusive judgements about farm forums in Ghana or anywhere in the world for that matter, a number of questions must first be considered.

First, is the radio farm-forum format intended only for a specific time period in a country's development? In other words, is the format as described in this article valid, say for a period of one to three years, after which it must change and adapt to varying social structures, a new set of logistics, different farm problems, advancing technology which may require diminishing dependence on a forum?

Second, if the format is not a static structure but a dynamic one, can we envisage the changes that a forum will have to go through and the broadcasting techniques and styles that have to adapt accordingly? What would some of these changes be? Or after a period, is the forum programme to be dropped and forgotten?

Third, whose role is it to organize, finance and manage the forums? Is forum work the role of the production unit, an agricultural agency, or a co-ordinated activity of several concerned sectors?

These questions are prompted by the development of forums in Ghana. When radio forums were in the initial pilot-project stage, all kinds of support were available: broadcast time, studio and field equipment, transportation, radio production staff, field officers, researchers, support from high officials, international funding. But as soon as the pilot project was completed, six months later, international funding stopped, researchers went back to their respective universities, field officers were taken back to their central urban offices, transportation and support logistics diminished, and the whole burden of organizing, expanding and financing the forums fell on the shoulders of the radio production staff who, in addition, had other broadcasting duties to perform. While the number of organized forums increased rapidly in the first three to four years, the growth since then has been static, although a modest target of 500 forums has been set. As the years went by, there was less and less support and involvement from the original co-ordinating development agencies. If growth appears to have been limited, it is because we have tried to encourage stable forums that will continually engage in their own autonomous activities, rather than fizzle out after their first attempts, and because in view of the reduced support, forum expansion has to be accommodated within the capabilities of the personnel and facilities of the radio production unit.

The first and second questions address themselves to the permanence of the radio farm forum as a format. They are asked especially in the context of Canada's dropping the format after several successful years, and the apparently diminishing interest in the forum in other countries, with some exceptions. Definitely there will be changes in topics, method of presentation, and general broadcast approach. As roads are built, mail services improved, urban centres established, fertilizer and farm products more available, higher literacy and educational levels reached and television competes for attention, the radio programme content and style will have to become proportionately more sophisticated. But will the concept and organization of forums also become increasingly unnecessary? The answer to this question will depend very much on the socio-economic milieu of the audience.

When the forum is organized along artificial lines or solely at the instigation of the radio programme, and with little other rationale, no amount of prodding and service from the radio station can keep these forums alive and active.

When the forums are based upon some already existing social grouping (the clan, the village, a group of farmers with common interests and goals), the forum will more likely be a permanent social organization in which the radio programme will eventually play an increasingly smaller role, more by way of providing information and catalysing activity, and less by way of nursing forums along and providing daily service by radio and field officers. In many ways, the permanence of a forum depends on the quality of the local leadership.

Accordingly, the style of the radio programme *vis-à-vis* these forums will become less 'dependence-oriented', though regular field visits help to maintain their interest and involvement. Radio would have to take a more active role in initiating new forums, but preferably within the already existing social and economic structures.

This in part answers the third question: whose role is it to organize, manage and finance forums? Though in many pilot projects, as in Ghana's case, the organizers were often a mix of development agencies and radio production personnel, it would seem that the real responsibility for organizing, managing and financing forums must be with the forums themselves. Radio, field officers and other development agencies may do their best to motivate, catalyse, assist, but unless forums realize their own responsibilities, they will never become viable or permanent. This is why in our broadcasts, we stress self-financing projects, group work and activity, assisting fellow forums in the region, and discussion, not only of short-term targets, but also long-term goals.

While it is true that in the beginning there should be a co-ordinated effort of the sectors concerned (radio, agriculture, social organizations), the forum planners and the radio production unit must also prepare for eventual disengagement and develop a more autonomous role for the forums.

In all the dialogue that may take place, either in the forums or on the radio, care must be taken to assure that the farmers' hopes and expectations are not raised beyond what is feasible. Many forums disintegrate because after discussion and preliminary local work, the needed response from government offices (roads, infrastructure, electrification, tractors, water pumps, etc.) is not forthcoming. Despite the reasons, valid or not, the rural broadcaster is often caught between supporting the people's demands and apologizing for government delay and inaction. If this happens too often, as it can, the programme tends to lose credibility and audience, and forums would naturally cease functioning. This is another reason for stressing the autonomous work of forums' self-financing, and self-benefiting activities.

As for the future, certainly there is need of more portable tape or cassette recorders of rugged durability, a service Land Rover (for autonomous planning of field trips, equipped with a medium-power VHF transceiver for mobile broadcasting and reporting), a researcher on the production team who can concentrate on background information and keep files up to date, agricultural training for the reporters/producers, modest print support (for calendars of events and programme guides) and occasional work seminars in order to exchange ideas on production and field approaches, possibly with radio forum personnel of other countries.

Simeon Bonzon

Cotabato now

We didn't have the flashy Toyota Land Cruisers that metropolitan stations had, nor their powerful VHF transceivers. Over the years I had to save to buy my own portable tape-recorder. There were no watertight job assignments. Everyone did everything—driving the Jeep, interviewing, editing, manning the console, even soldering circuits. But this is rural broadcasting.

Cotabato is a modern corruption of an ancient word, Kuta Wato, meaning the stone fort. In early Muslim history, there was once a stone fort in the city of Cotabato, capital of the province of Cotabato on Mindanao, the largest island in the Philippines. The very title of this rural programme, *Cotabato Ngayon* (or Cotabato now) provokes a paradox of old and new, of tradition and modernization, of ethnic folkways and the invasion of the city 'subcultures'. The old stone fort today is merely a legend, but Cotabato continues as a city and a province at the crossroads of development. Radio plays an important

The author, Simeon Bonzon, formerly senior radio producer at DXMS radio station, Cotabato City, Philippines, is now foreign news editor at the Bureau of National and Foreign Information, Ministry of Public Information.

role in their development: keeping the region informed, teaching the farmers new techniques, reporting weather and road conditions (landslides are common), and providing numerous services to the public.

This is the story of one radio programme of DXMS, broadcasting at 10 kW to Cotabato and the western Mindanao region.

The setting

The Philippines is an archipelago situated at the south-east rim of the Asian mainland. The more than 7,000 islands are grouped around the three largest: Luzon, Visayas and Mindanao. The southern-most island group, Mindanao, shares a centuries-old culture with the Muslim (called Moros by the Spaniards) sea-gypsies, who migrated in small boats from the Asian mainland and other archipelagic regions. Though the main ethnic strain in Cotabato is Maguindanaon, there are at least a dozen other distinct ethnic groups, each with its own language and culture.

Since the 1950s, there has been a major influx of settlers to Mindanao. These have come from various linguistic groups—Tagalog, Ilocano, Illonggo, Cebuano—comprising (with the Muslim groups) an audience extremely rich in cultural and linguistic differences.

In Cotabato, as in the rest of Mindanao, the Muslims established sultanates, which were further networked with the Datus (princes) of each major family group. The sultanate system was the religious, political, social, economic and familial focal point of all activity—a system that exists and thrives today, despite the inroads of 'Western-oriented democracy' and its governmental institutions.

Though the southern Philippines was once the sole dominion of the Muslims, the new settlers, mainly Christian, are now the more populous group. This has caused a number of evident changes: loyalty to a central government, based in Manila, the growth of urbanization and a money economy, establishment of a formal school system, the spread of large business enterprises, trade and commerce. What is less obvious is how these new changes have affected the Muslim way of life, for their traditional culture is in evidence everywhere: the sultan and *datu* systems, their language and attire (many men still carry their *kris*, the curly-bladed sword), their brass-ware and artefacts, the sculptured motifs on their swift outriggers, their loyalty to the basic tenets of Islam.

Mindanao, the second largest island in the Philippines (57,000 square kilometres), has the highest peak (Mount Apo), the second largest river system (Rio Grande de Mindanao) and the deepest suboceanic gorge in the Pacific—the famous Mindanao Deep. Climate (salubrious and bracing), rainfall (regular and evenly distributed throughout the year) and the location of Mindanao outside the typhoon path, combine to provide the fullest variety of tropical and citrus fruits. Despite the fact that more than half the country's agricultural exports are produced here, this island as a whole lags behind the other two regions in modernization.

Mindanao shares the same broadcasting system with the rest of the Philippines—a system unique to Asia. Since 1931, more than 250 private (most of them commercial) stations have proliferated throughout the country, leaving only a marginal role for the State-owned network. Though most stations are located in Luzon, and especially in the Manila area, there are more than forty in Mindanao, ranging from 1 kW to 10 kW in power. This dispersion of low- to medium-powered transmitters has led to very highly localized programming, mainly in the vernacular languages. One community station broadcasts in twelve languages.

But while the avidity for advertising revenue has spurred the establishment of scores of radio stations all over the country, it has also taken its toll in terms of mush 'soap operas', banal D.J. programmes, and hard-sell advertisements, most of which are totally unrelated to the development needs of the region.

On the other side of the balance, commercialism has succeeded in marketing transistor radios far and wide. Conservative estimates put radio households at 80 per cent; many areas, especially near urban centres have more than 95 per cent radio households.

DXMS: the radio station

When the Oblate Missionary Fathers came to Cotabato in 1939, they launched an ambitious social programme which included two major schools, a housing programme, the weekly newspaper, *Mindanao Cross*, now the largest regional weekly and, in 1958, two radio stations, DXMS and DXND.[1]

Although DXMS is a privately owned church-oriented station, it accepts revenue for commercial advertising. Programming has followed the general format of commercial stations, except for the increased proportion of informational public service and other developmental programmes. The sister station, DXND, being completely non-commercial, has an even wider range of informational and developmental programmes geared specifically to local problems, local subcultures, and the dozen dialects spoken in the immediate coverage area.

DXMS programmes for a wide variety of ethnic groups and new settlers. *Cotabato Ngayon* inherited the audience of its predecessor, 'Apyong the Mighty' (in real life, Neps Dimacutac), a comic personality, whose home-spun humour reached all classes of society in three languages: Chabacano, for the Zamboanga provinces; Maranao, for the Lanao Lake region; and Ilonggo, for Visayan settlers in most of the provinces of western Mindanao.

Transmitting at 10kW, DXMS has the edge on rival stations and captures the largest audiences during most time slots.

The production unit

The team was composed of four: two reporter-producers (one of whom doubled as driver and technician), one studio announcer and one continuity/master control tech-

1. *D* represents the call letter for the Philippines, *X* stands for Mindanao, *MS* (the larger station, 10 kW) stands for Mindanao-Sulu, and *ND* (1 kW) stands for Notre-Dame.

nician. None had been formally trained for this kind of work, but learned on the job. That was also why the team was extremely versatile. Almost anyone could do the other's job, except for the master control. All were station personnel who had other responsibilities: production supervision, staff announcing, and station management.

Field-production facilities included: an old Jeep that was renovated and fitted with a two-way VHF radio and one portable tape-recorder. For studio production and airing we used the mixing console at the master studio which had: two turntables, two tape-recorders, one recorder, one tape-recorder, two semi-professional recorders, one cassette deck and a telephone patch.

With this set-up, *Cotabato Ngayon*, could programme studio reports, studio discussions, telephone calls, pretaped and edited actualities (from any of the six recorders) and mobile reports from the two-way radio. Additional two-way radios would have widened the coverage area for on-air reporting.

The entire cost of the programme (personnel, facilities, and operations) was covered by the station as its public service contribution. It should be stressed that the programme itself was not directly sponsored, though commercial advertisements were placed before and after the major station breaks.

The programme

When Neps Dimacutac (producer/announcer of the original magazine programme) died in a motor accident in 1966, the DXMS staff met to discuss ways to maintain the public service and entertainment following of 'Apyong the Mighty'. The station management wanted a format that would be flexible, informative, and public-service oriented. The time slot was 07.15 to 08.00 hours, immediately after the national and world news round-up—the peak listening time.

In brief the objectives of the new programme were: (a) to keep the people informed of local, national and world events; (b) to report in depth on selected news events, especially those affecting the local community;

(c) to provide public-service announcements and assistance as flexibly as possible; (d) to provide on-location reporting of important events, festivals and other occasions; (e) to reflect people's views through field reports and *vox populi*; (f) to catalyse and spur development projects through the use of mobile facilities of the programme; (g) to promote a sense of community.

Since the audience was pre-eminently heterogeneous, the production unit had to be constantly aware of the dozen and more ethnic and language groups of the listeners. Most of the staff announcers, fortunately, were multilingual. The programme itself was prepared in Pilipino, the national language, but often glided easily into Chabacano, Ilonggo, Cebuano, Maguinadanao or English, depending on the topic and specific audience to be reached.

Though not formally a news programme, *Cotabato Ngayon* used the following sources: monitored radio news programmes from Manila; local and national newspapers; bulletins from the various mayors and provincial government officials; phone calls from various agencies, offices and institutions. It may be surprising to outsiders, but in small towns it is quite natural for anyone to report events or ask for public-service announcements from the local radio station. These announcements included such things as: reports of landslides and delayed buses; lost *carabaos* and strayed farm animals; deceased relatives (family ties and traditions require the members, no matter where they are, to come and console the bereaved family); arrival of relatives in a distant town. In a territory where telegrams are expensive and telephones non-existent outside the urban centres, radio is the poor-man's telephone and telegraph.

From the various reports and bulletins, we could often prepare programming a month in advance, but always being flexible to provide for impromptu events and unforeseen happenings. Over the years, the reporters cultivated credibility and contacts, and were often called upon by various members of the community to make announcements or cover events.

The regional, weekly, *Mindanao Cross*, provided a one-eighth page, free advertisement for the programme and often wrote up our radio interviews for a news article. Throughout the eighteen-hour broadcast day, *Cotabato Ngayon* received regular 'plugs'.

Since the *Mindanao Cross* is issued only weekly, *Cotabato Ngayon* sought to provide solid, positive, developmental information during the intervening six days.

The format

Basically, the programme consisted of a talk format utilizing as many sources as possible: mobile reports, phone calls, taped current events, studio reports and discussions. When major events took place outside the air time, these were pre-recorded and edited for insertion in the morning programme. Material for hard news was, of course, prepared immediately for the next newscast.

The programme outline was prepared the day before and anchored by the studio announcer, who aired the inputs in the agreed sequence, always providing the necessary continuity, mostly non-scripted.

A typical one-hour programme sequence would be as follows:

Station identification
News round-up
Cotobato theme and line-up
Mobile reports
Taped actualities and phone calls
Community announcements
Studio messages/interviews
Wrap-up and closing
Station identification/commercials.

When two or more events took place during the morning slot, the mobile unit covered one event, while a separate team covered the other, with the portable tape-recorder. The reports with the current events were edited for insertion during the programme, or the report was phoned in during the broadcast.

A favourite scene for mobile reports was Cotabato airport, the hub of most contact with Manila, the seat of all national events. The mobile team interviewed government officials, institution directors and personalities to ascertain the latest happenings and to preview coming events; mayors seeking national funds for public-works projects, university deans attending international conferences, local delegates representing provincial and regional interests in the national assembly.

A more localized source of provincial news was the bus terminal and bus rides to various towns and provinces along the coast or deep into the interior.

Major routes go as far as Davao, Iligan City, Cagayan de Oro and Zamboanga, taking from five to twelve hours or more. Smaller buses and renovated passenger Jeeps (called 'jeepneys') cover the small towns in the province of Cotabato. In a region where there are no railways and air travel is expensive, it is not surprising to find heavy traffic on provincial roads.

A chat with the bus driver or conductor usually revealed road and weather conditions, and news from other towns. The frequent stops (for lunch, refuelling, picking-up passengers and frequent breakdowns) provided opportunities to interview both passengers and people from the vicinity. Alert reporters could get a good summary of changing prices from town to town, shortages of rice or other food items, the effects of drought or heavy rains on the expected crop output. Urgent news could be phoned in from the next town having a telephone; other interviews were edited upon return for incorporation as segments in the next day's programme. It should also be recalled that most routes cover territory with extremely varying ethnic groups and languages. While these interviews could form exciting programme matter, the reporter had to be familiar with the dialects spoken or choose as universal a language as possible. He also had to be aware of particular local customs and sometimes shyness which made difficult a smooth, interesting conversation.

Cotabato Ngayon also assisted other DXMS developmental programmes. On an earlier time slot in 1967, DXMS aired a 'Farmers' School of the Air', which included the launching of a communal irrigation system to be established in Tacurong, a town several hundred kilometres from Cotabato City.

Months before the actual launching, which was to be inaugurated by the Executive Secretary to the President, the mobile team interviewed key persons in the town, who voiced their support for the project. These interviews were aired regularly together with up-dated bulletins and feedback mail.

On launching day itself, *Cotabato Ngayon* had its microphones ready for reports, interviews and coverage of the inauguration speech by the then Secretary, Rafael Salas, who spoke in English, Pilipino and Visayan. As a result, the whole town turned out, tools in hand, to dig the irrigation canals. Overall, the excitement of the first day drew more workers during the week of canal digging. As a result, the irrigation canal was completed ahead of schedule.

Evaluation

There has been no formal evaluation of *Cotabato Ngayon*, nor of any of the DXMS programmes. Formal research in rural towns is a luxury we can ill afford. The station does receive regular ratings from commercial surveys, but these are mainly to inform advertisers of popular programmes and stations for their publicity outlets.

But, actually, the programme format provided its own feedback. Through telephone calls, letters, interviews and mobile reports, the production unit was constantly in touch with one or other segment of the audience. It was like an open nerve continuously pulsing with news and information from the immediate area and from the region (through monitored news programmes).

Observations

Though the format was workable and the programme successful, despite its limitations in equipment and manpower, the production team faced a number of problems which could be solved positively:

The programme would need at least three rugged vehicles each with powerful transceivers, in order to penetrate the deeper areas of the region and provide a more region-wide coverage. Additional portable tape-recorders or high-quality cassette recorders (at least one for each reporter) would give more flexibility in the field.

There is need of local training on the seminar level to work out specific strategies and approaches to link radio more closely to development projects.

Aside from additional mobile reporters, there would be need of a production-research assistant, who could prepare data on technical activities to be covered and information sheets for *ad lib* scripts, edit archive tapes for historical occasions and assist generally on all script and tape needs for the programme.

There should be some way of collaborating with mobile reporters of other stations in Mindanao (and indeed other islands in the archipelago) for multi-point coverages and dissemination of reports from other areas (especially during times of disaster, such as earthquakes, tidal waves heavy rains, landslides—all of which are common throughout the islands), but the commercial system of broadcasting and the stiff competition for limited advertising revenue block any efforts in this direction. An independent station, unfortunately, has to operate independently. Certain networks do manage to produce simulcasts, but low-power, single-side band systems and bad weather conditions prevent clear reception. Satellite is a possibility, but there will inevitably be problems of cost, access and allocation of channels, especially for the independent local stations.

With or without the above improvements, the key asset of *Cotabato Ngayon* is its flexible format: live reports, telephone calls, taped current events, and studio sources. It can adapt to meet almost any developmental need: providing information, instructing in farm techniques, catalysing development projects, focusing on issues, mustering personal support, assisting in disasters, and keeping people in contact with each other. The programme has a vital role to fulfil, not in being a passive spectator to development, but as an active participant in the development of the region.

Hernando Bernal Alarcon

Radio for the *campesinos*

The first audience of Radio Sutatenza, in 1947 when it was founded, was formed by two old ladies who were seized with fright when they listened to a radio for the first time in their lives.

Desiring to reach the campesinos *by radio, Monsignor José Joaquín Salcedo packed a radio set and batteries on a mule and trekked up a hill near Sutatenza, a remote hamlet in Colombia. His Jesuit brother helped him build a makeshift transmitter housed in a bisuit tin.*

One Sunday morning, the assistant turned on the radio so the campesinos *could hear Father Salcedo's sermon. Upon hearing the familiar voice, the two old ladies looked for Father Salcedo, but could not find him.*

That is an old story. Today, almost every *campesino* owns a radio and listens to it almost all day long. The home-made transmitter of Radio Sutatenza has now developed into an entire network comprising five radio stations. Over the years, the network has not only orginated

The author, Hernando Bernal Alarcon, is director of the *campaña de procreación responsable* organized under the auspices of the Acción Cultural Popular, Bogotá, Colombia.

religious programmes, but has also covered social well-being, literacy, economic co-operatives, adult education and, recently, responsible parenthood.

Setting

Colombia is located at the north-western corner of South America. The Andes mountain range cuts right through the western half and slopes downwards to huge plains and virgin forests in the east. As the country is right on the Equator, temperatures can range from near freezing in the higher mountains to tropical warmth in the lowlands. The country is also fortunate in having coastlines on both the Pacific Ocean and the Caribbean Sea.

About half of Colombia's 25 million people are engaged in agricultural occupations, though this sector of the labour force produces only one-quarter of the country's total income. The main farm products include: maize, cassava, coffee, rice and bananas.

Some farmers own their own small plots, though many work as day labourers for other farms or plantations. Because life is generally hard in the rural areas, *campesinos* have developed several other skills, mainly self-taught: cattle-raising, fishing, mining, handicrafts, and doing odd jobs in nearby towns.

Terrain, language, ethnic customs over the centuries have tended to isolate the *campesinos*. With isolation, tradition has often set in to make acceptance of change a slow and difficult process. While Spanish influence brought Christianity, it is for the *campesinos* a religion mixed with ancient customs and rituals, often bordering on what the outsider might term magic or superstition.

Socially, people are modest, even prudish by Western standards. Words pertaining to sex are seldom used in polite conversation and certain actions or reactions are closely guided by set taboos. In contrast, there is among many men a strong sense of *machismo* or an exaggerated sense of man's superiority over woman.

In a country where children are counted as both a social blessing (not to speak of a religious blessing) and an economic asset, it is not surprising that Colombia has one of the highest population growth rates in the world: 3.2 per cent. And yet there are many children who are born unwanted, whose social and economic survival is at risk both while they are young and later as adult members of the community. For example, when the half of the nation that today is 15 years old or younger comes of age, they will certainly face an uncertain future, whether it be lands to farm or jobs to hunt for in the towns. Besides the situational and historical factors of terrain, language, ethnic customs, religion and isolation, there is also the problem of ignorance due to lack of information.

It is in this complex setting that the Acción Cultural Popular launched its project on responsible parenthood, utilizing all means of communication at its disposal, but especially radio.

Organization of the project

Acción Cultural Popular (ACPO) is an autonomous institution which administers an adult-education programme for the *campesinos*, a radio network, a newspaper and several publications, and a regional network of *campesino* field training institutes. It is a non-commercial organization, though operational costs are partially offset through paid advertisements on radio or in the various publications. Donations from the government, various foundations and international organizations have helped to build much of the infrastructure that exists today.

Under ACPO, a special project for responsible parenthood (*campaña de procreación responsable*) was organized. The director of the project has prime responsibility for the philosophy, strategy, and co-ordination of the various programmes. He prepares articles for the weekly magazine, *El Campesino*; supervises and edits the radio scripts, so as to assure relevance of materials to the overall goals of the project; liaises with other ACPO writers and scripters so as to maintain unity in the overall programming of the station and to minimize programme materials that might go counter to the overall campaign.

An administrator co-ordinates the implementation of all related tasks: submission of materials, preparation of contracts, production schedules, accounting and evaluation reports of programmes or articles.

Two secretaries assist in the administrative and clerical duties. This four-man team is supported by ACPO as a total institution: access to production facilities and air time, publication space, the services of various media practitioners, and the co-ordination of the field workers or *auxiliars*. ACPO has not only its own radio network (with transmitters in Bogotá, Cali, Barranquilla, Medillín and Magangué) and printing presses, but also a master disc cutter, an audio-visual production unit, mobile audio-visual units (called ACPOMOBILE), and a mobile print unit.

The programme

Since ACPO has been administering educational programmes on radio and in the newspaper for several years, and has covered topics such as the family, parenthood and human rights, the campaign in many respects was not completely new. What the campaign did was to intensify ACPO's concentration on these issues and open up discussions on sex education—previously considered taboo as a topic for radio or newspapers.

The basic assumption underlying the project was that the *campesinos* were insufficiently informed. Without complete information and knowledge of the alternatives, parents could hardly decide rationally on the size of their family or on the methods for spacing or limiting the number of children. Thus ACPO's basic philosophy of procreation was that the planning of a family, in fact of every single birth, must be the result of a wise decision. The *campaña de procreación responsable* would gear its forces towards providing the correct information to make that decision.

On radio only two basic formats were used: the spot and the drama. The spots were brief messages of twenty to sixty seconds each aired every half-hour or hour between 05.00 and 24.00 hours. These messages were aimed at provoking questions rather than answering them—questions that would be handled by the regional field workers and trainers, through correspondence or in more detailed newspaper articles. The spots were scripted as a set of six and changed every few months with a new set. A sample of a drama spot can be found on page 64.

To reinforce motivation and understanding, the fifteen-minute drama was selected as the format. The series, entitled *Viva la Vida* (Live Life) and aired daily except Saturday and Sunday, centred on a typical *campesino* family. Using real-life situations and typical characters, the series touched on basic attitudes, customs, motivations, behaviour related to procreation and responsible parenthood. The director reviewed all scripts and taped dramas to assure continuity of theme and constant reinforcing of the desired attitudes and values. These dramas (which now number more than 120 in the series) were aired daily from Monday to Friday. As can be seen from some of the scripts (excerpts on page 65), some of the programmes dealt quite candidly with sensitive subjects.

Programme support

The campaign has to be seen in its totality, of which radio was only one, though a significant, part. For both the drama spots and the drama series *Viva la Vida*, there were also jingles (see sample on page 66) and short one-sentence 'stingers' scheduled at appropriate programme breaks.

On the print side, a book entitled *Sex and Marriage* was prepared by a group of specialists and given free to more than 100,000 *campesinos*. A second edition is being sold at an extremely modest price. The weekly newspaper *El Campesino* has already published more than 200 articles on general and specific aspects of responsible parenthood. Occasionally, special issues carried a four-page folded insert which the readers could remove and keep separately. Some of the letters of the *campesinos*, which pose questions about the campaign, were also published in the paper.

Posters, distributed to strategic public places, strengthened various motivational aspects of the campaign with both drawings and a brief message.

Finally, the *campesino* field trainers were also instrumental in teaching various aspects of the programme in their respective adult-education groups. They also served to provide direct information and motivation, as well as to prompt their trainees to write further questions to the campaign headquarters in Bogotá. More than 12,000 letters have been received and answered, either in the newspaper or within the radio programmes.

Evaluation

From the beginning, evaluation was organized to provide feedback information on letters received concerning the campaign, evaluation of the book *Sex and Marriage*, and the effectiveness of the courses held at the regional *campesino* training institutes. In 1975, a formal evaluation research of the project was conducted and reproduced.

In general, the research has shown that, in the early stages of the campaign, a significant proportion of negative reactions and comments were received. As the campaign progressed, it came to be more acceptable. But as later radio programmes did not provide any specific information regarding the means for population control, the motivation to send letters of inquiry diminished and fewer letters were received.

The information coming from these letters could have been helpful in guiding the scriptwriters, if there had been some method of providing them with this information in a brief form and in a way to stimulate corrective action.

One thing the programmes have certainly achieved is to discuss openly and candidly very sensitive topics, such as sex, marriage and parental responsibility in the context of a society steeped in tradition, where the word sex itself is taboo.

Sample drama spot

Audio effects—street sounds: horns, motors, voices

FELIPE: [Surprise] Manuel! When did you arrive?
MANUEL: Felipe! It's been so long! I've just arrived, but *you* have forgotten your home town!
FELIPE: Where are you going to stay?

MANUEL: No! I'm *not* staying. I'm leaving today. I don't like the city; it frightens me. Look, there on the sidewalk. . . .

FELIPE: What? I don't see anything!

Audio effects—'stinger'

MALE VOICE: As a matter of fact, all day long, Manuel has seen several children sleeping on the sidewalk. This is not new for Felipe. He sees them every day. . . . Everywhere, dirty, abandoned, sad children.

FEMALE VOICE: Thousands of children die of hunger and cold all over the world. Think about it before you have the next child.

Excerpts from *Viva la Vida*

Rivalry among Brothers, by Rodolfo Gómez

NARRATOR: Manuel turned pale and his hands began to shake. It was not the first time he had heard such a thing. His son, Octavio, was totally irresponsible, like a wild wolf preying on tame lambs.

OCTAVIO: What is the matter, papa?

MANUEL: [Severe] What have you done to Juana's daughter?

OCTAVIO: [Tense] What have they told you?

MANUEL: [Angry] You know what!

OCTAVIO: I don't know. But it's the most common thing in the world!

MANUEL: So, you think it is *normal* to seduce a simple *campesina*?

OCTAVIO: I didn't seduce her, papa. She did it willingly. I didn't hurt her. On the contrary . . .

MANUEL: [Vehement] You rascal! How do you dare say that?

OCTAVIO: [Trying to calm] Yes, yes, papa. Don't worry! It's nothing serious.

MANUEL: She is pregnant! You will have a son! You will be his father.

OCTAVIO: No. . . . *She* will be his *mother*. I'm not marrying her and I won't ever get married.

MANUEL: [Wrathful] You seducer, I am going to disinherit you!

OCTAVIO: But why? Is it *my* fault? It's not for men to worry about! It's her fault for not taking care . . . you know!

MANUEL: Shut up! You make me sick! But I assure you: I am still your father and you will have to be responsible for your acts. *You will have to take care of the child!*

Music bridge

Sample of a recorded song

A song that tries to counter the traditional, often exaggerated notion that having many children brings automatic prosperity.

Los Cuentos de mi Abuela Pepa
(Stories of Grandma Pepa), by Jorge Jiménez B.

> Grandma Pepa used to say
> A long, long time ago
> That God gave us children
> All with bread under their arms.
>
> With this hopeful inspiration
> Papa and Mama gave birth to *ten* of us
> But poor old papa and dear mama,
> They worked so hard to raise us.
>
> Then I fell in love,
> And married Pedro Pablo
> And since then
> More than seven years have passed.
>
> We remember well Grandma Pepa's story
> And so we had Luisito,
> And then Jacinto, and then Clemencia
> And after them the baby, Pablito.
>
> We love our *four* children
> And we want them to go to school and live well.
> But before we have another,
> We will surely think twice.

Jaroslav Košťál

Rural broadcasting in Czechoslovakia

As the rural situation in Czechoslovakia has changed vastly over the last fifty years, so too has rural broadcasting. The old categories no longer fit. Most farmers today have radio, many watch television, most have books and read widely.

Many people in rural areas live and work in towns, though they listen regularly to 'rural programmes'. Whereas earlier rural programmes stressed basic production and collective farming, today's rural broadcaster must be both an agricultural specialist and an effective communicator.

The Czechoslovak Socialist Republic comprises almost 80,000 square kilometres of land, about half of which is arable soil. Fertile zones are spread over the plains and threaded by numerous rivers. Low mountains, seldom over 2,000 metres above sea level, border the country and are also found in an inland range in Slovakia. A network of tarmacadamed roads provides access to most places.

Most of the country's 15 million people consist of two nations: the Czechs and the Slovaks. Culturally, these

The author, Jaroslav Košťál, is head of the Department of Research, Radio Czechoslovakia, Prague, Czechoslovakia.

two nations are very similar, with only slight differences in language. There are also about 100,000 other people belonging to other national groups: Poles, Hungarians and Germans. These have their own educational system, press, and regional broadcasting in their respective native language.

Today, about a million people work in the rural sector of the economy, or about 15 per cent of the labour force. This represents only about one-third of the pre-1939 rural labour force and shows not only a significant mobility within this social group, but also a dynamic change in the very structure of labour and production and in the strategy of land utilization in Czechoslovakia.

In the first phase of socialization, 1949–59, farmers established agricultural co-operatives and used collective farming methods for crop and livestock production. In those days, the average farm size was between 200 and 300 hectares.

In the second phase, 1960–75, the agricultural co-operatives pooled together to economize resources and adapt new technology to farming needs.

In the third phase, lands were even more concentrated. Co-operative farms today average 2,200 hectares, while State farms average 7,100 hectares. This has led to the creation of more complex organizations with a high degree of specialization and integration to relate farm production to marketing and trade outlets. Thus, today, 95 per cent of all lands are socialized under the 1,908 co-operative farms or the 194 State farms.

This concentration of resources has helped the country to gain self-sufficiency in livestock production. The immediate aim now is to achieve self-sufficiency in grain production. This has been made somewhat difficult by the general decline in workable farm area by 10 per cent since 1936. None the less, the total volume of production has increased by 40 per cent since 1936 and by 4.8 per cent annually since 1968. But to continue this growth pattern and eventually achieve self-sufficiency in food production will require an intense efficiency in farming. Doubtless, radio is seen as a key catalyst in this operation.

Target audience

The main audience of the rural programmes is the million or so Czech and Slovak farmers, though the latter can also hear programmes broadcast from Bratislava, the capital of Slovakia. Of this group about 70 per cent are regular listeners. The total audience includes residents of large urban centres, who tune in to the programme for various types of current and technical information. Surveys between 1974 and 1977 have shown that about 60 per cent of listeners are women, about 40 per cent are over 60. It should also be noted that rural residents also listen to other types of radio programme.

Statistical reports in 1973 show that the rural labour force comprises: 25,000 university graduates, 100,000 who have completed secondary studies, and 220,000 skilled agricultural or forestry professionals. This does not include hundreds of researchers who are employed by the Czechoslovak Rural Academy (founded in 1923), or qualified engineers and veterinarians who seek work in agricultural fields. Since 1975, the Ministry of Agriculture and Food Production has set up specialized rural institutes in all of the ten regions of Czechoslovakia.

Two-, three- and four-year courses have been designed at the secondary level in specialized fields relevant to each region. The first class will graduate in 1978. While the majority of the rural labour force comprises low- to medium-skilled or self-taught farmers, this social sector is rapidly changing to become more educated, more technically skilled, more culturally exposed, and thereby more information-concious.

Nine out of ten households have television and it is widely watched from 19.30 to 21.00 hours. Almost all families have a radio, at least a portable transistor set. Eight out of ten families have their own books, 40 per cent have personal libraries of more than fifty volumes. As high as 95 per cent of the rural population read a daily newspaper; half go to the cinema at least once a year.

The rural population is also an increasingly younger group. The present median age is between 39 and 44, but this figure must be interpreted in the context of a labour force in which one-fifth continues working even beyond post-productive age—55 for women, 61 for men.

Not having the easy access to cinema, dance parties, and other cultural amusements available in the cities, rural folk tend to rely more heavily on radio and television as forms of entertainment and sources of information.

Village settlements are no smaller than 2,000 inhabitants, unlike the typically smaller hamlets of yesteryear. Many are grouped around larger, more diversified urban centres, thus providing for increased social mobility and cultural exposure. Even within a single family, there may be a farmer, a technician, a town worker and so on. Rural families today are no longer homogeneous, isolated, tradition-bound. The peasant no longer lives on the margin of society or culture.

Broadcasting in Czechoslovakia

Radio Czechoslovakia, originally established as a private enterprise, broadcast its first programmes on 15 May 1923 at the very dawn of the era of radio. Specialized rural broadcasts followed soon after on 3 January 1926. These first programmes sought to form a communication link between the country's cultural centres and the various scattered villages. They provided information on animal husbandry, crop cultivation and basic poultry production. But in those early days less than 5 per cent of the farmers had access to a radio, at that time the large, expensive vacuum-tube set.

After the Second World War, radio came under the management of the State and the number of licenses rapidly increased, especially during the 1960s. Rural programmes were then oriented to post-1945 economic reconstruction and to assist in the first phase of socialized agriculture: the formation of co-operatives and the establishment of collective farming systems.

During the second phase of the socialization programme, radio sought to accelerate the diffusion of newly developing farm techniques and machinery. Contests aimed at solving farm problems were organized. Among the results were 240 new technological projects and machine designs now currently in use in many of the agricultural co-operatives. Television too has focused national attention on the life and work of the farmers, changing conditions, and how the modern farmer has had to adapt to these changes.

During the present third phase, the role of radio has become increasingly technical and specialized: to assist in the nation's accelerated production plan. This includes the promotion of scientific farm management and the relations of the farm production sector with marketing, trade, and related industries.

The programme is broadcast on medium wave, 638 kHz and relayed on 1484 kHz from Brno. It is also broadcast on VHF 66.32 MHz from the regional station in Ostrava.

Radio Czechoslovakia is non-commercial. Its operating revenue is derived from individual licence fees and various publicity spots for socialist enterprises. All financial income and expenditure are controlled by the National Budget Office.

The programme

For the last twelve years, the programme, simply called *Rural Broadcast* has been aired for fifteen minutes at midday, Monday to Friday. The general programme sequence is as follows: 12.00 hours, popular music; 12.30 hours, national and international news; 12.45 hours, *Rural Broadcast*; 13.00 hours, programme review; 13.03 hours, classical music (Dvořák, Smetana, Novák, Glazunov, etc.).

Since 1975, the programme has become more or less fixed in a magazine format: signature tune; brief review of the topic of the day; music bridge; information magazine of the day; music bridge; closing.

On Mondays, the programme focuses on long-term objectives of rural production, trade and specific problems in raw materials and energy resources. Short-term campaigns are generally avoided, but when necessary these *ad hoc* tasks are related to the overall long-term objectives.

It has been found over the years that the magazine format is the most flexible, adaptable to almost any type of programme material. It can be a commentary, taped discussion, edited interview, taped current events, or any combination of inputs. As a rule, the programme acts as a forum for sharing the experiences of rural scientists, experts and officials; for identifying village and national problems; for airing ideas on the relations between the farm sector and trade, industry, and the economic community in general. Using interviews with people on the street or on the farm, the programme tries to personalize its approach towards inducing efficient work habits, conservation of energy and natural resources. With its vast resources of information, the programme also disseminates information on new techniques and technology.

When the programme was applied to the overall national development plan to concentrate farm production units and achieve self-sufficiency, preparation included: analysis of social and cultural transmission; analysis of the changes needed in farming techniques; planning of ways and means to instruct on new techniques; preparing for the social and economic changes needed in transition from many medium-sized farm units to fewer but larger units; conveying the new management techniques needed for these social and economic reforms; pinpointing the links and providing the necessary liaison between production and markets.

The production team

The rural broadcasting staff of Radio Czechoslovakia is composed of six people—all women! Of these, two are graduates in rural science, and one in journalism. The Chief of the Unit directs and organizes the production of all programmes; four staff members assist in the conception of specific programmes and the scripting; the fifth performs secretarial and administrative duties. All, except the secretary, have been trained in announcing and often voice their own scripts, though on occasion they may recruit outside talent. Under the direction of the chief, each of the producer/editors may undertake special assignments or programmes.

As the team is part of Radio Czechoslovakia, they have access to the production facilities of the station. These include Tesla Elektroakustika mixing consoles and Studer professional tape-recorders and cassette decks. In the field, producers use Uher 4000 portable tape-recorders and Uher 210CR cassette recorders. In addition, mobile vans are equipped with Siemens control amplifiers, Elektroakustika or Studer mixers, and Studer recorders. On occasion, some programmes are simulcast with programme sources originating in both Prague and Bratislava.

In the preparation of programmes, producers and scripters have access to several periodicals and studies, especially research reports of the Academy of Rural Science and prognostic studies on rural and industrial areas. Within the Union of Czech Journalists, there is a Club of Rural Journalists which organizes press conferences, seminars, and study visits. The club also disseminates rural information and facilitates contacts with technical specialists. Participation in rural technology trade fairs in the U.S.S.R., the German Democratic Republic and Bulgaria provide not only current information, but also programme material for the rural producers. Extensive use is also made of cable lines and telex to obtain on short notice updated scientific information, as will be seen in the programme excerpts.

Through the Centre for Education and Staff Training of Radio Czechoslovakia, all broadcasters are encouraged to undertake periodic in-service training and further education.

Evaluation

The rural broadcasts are fortunate to have regular evaluation by the Department of Research of Radio Czechoslovakia and by the Methods and Research Cabinet in Bratislava. These two groups also undertake in-depth studies and special surveys, often with the assistance of rural experts. The results of these studies are then reviewed by external social scientists and published.

In addition, the broadcast team often solicits the opinions of the audience at trade fairs, interviews and other location recordings.

Excerpts of a typical programme

(After signature and opening remarks.)

Audio effects—sound of tractor, fade under

MODERATOR: Summer is nearing and in a few weeks the first tractors will move into the fields. Sheafs of grain will gently bow before the mowers, and we hope for an abundant harvest.

Audio effects—fade up tractor sound and fade

MODERATOR: Yes, summer is nearing and the next crop is one more step towards our country's goal: self-sufficiency in grain production. But we hope that we can keep our grain losses to a minimum. We asked Mr Jaroslav Skolil from the Ministry of Agriculture and Food Production, just how grain losses can affect our goal of self-sufficiency.

Tape

MR JAROSLAV: If we wish to achieve self-sufficiency, we must solve the problem of grain losses. In a normal year, losses are about 2 per cent, but if the weather is bad, losses can increase to 3 per cent and higher. Now you may think that this is very little. But you must understand that even only 1 per cent of the total crop is already 70,000 tons of grain! If these 70,000 tons of grain were milled, they would supply 6 per cent of our annual food needs. This is the importance of trying to save even that 2 per cent of grain loss.

MODERATOR: Mr Skolil also suggested a very effective way to reduce grain losses. This is to use an indicator.

STUDIO ANNOUNCER 1 (*in slow, explanatory tone of voice*): An indicator is an electronic device that shows the optimum speed of a harvester machine at which the loss of grain can be kept to a minimum. The indicator is being developed by the Agricultural Machines Workshop in Dašice, the Research Institute of Agricultural Techniques in Prague, and the Tesla-Pardubice Institute of Radio Electronic Research in Opočinek.

Audio effects—sound of teleprinter and fade

MODERATOR: Our colleague, Pavel Kačer, just telexed this message from the Agricultural Machines Workshop in Bohemia.

STUDIO ANNOUNCER 2 (*reading telex*): In 1976, we started large-scale production of indicators in Dašice. We finished 1,200 indicators before harvest time and 1,800 just after the harvest. Next year we will manufacture 1,800 indicators before harvest time. By the following year, we should be able to supply the needs of the entire country, and perhaps start preparing for servicing foreign requests.

MODERATOR: The indicator is an electronic device which requires precision installation, maintenance and handling; I talked to the chief of the production workshop in Dašice, Mr Vladimir Drátek.

Tape

MR VLADIMIR DRÁTEK: Our factory has seventeen production workshops in Czechoslovakia. These workshops guarantee the proper function of these indicators, they install them on the harvesters, they service them as necessary, and train harvester operators how to use them.

Music bridge—a short typical folk melody
from southern Moravia

MODERATOR: That well-known melody now takes us to southern Moravia where there is a Machine and Tractor Station in Znojmo. Mr Makovsty, you operate the E–512 harvester and I notice you also use an indicator. What has been your experience with this indicator and how accurate has it been in showing losses of grain?

Tape

MR MAKOVSKY (*in Znojmo*): Humm, my experience with the indicator has been very good. I tried it last year for the first time in the Mostava co-operative in Galanta where I was harvesting barley. While operating the harvester, I tried to keep the running speed so that the dial stayed within the yellow range. After one run, I checked for losses. There were none. But the harvest output was high. I couldn't believe it. So I tried it again, this time increasing the running speed so that the dial moved within the green range. But there were a lot of losses. In general, I think the indicator is a good device and when used correctly can prevent loss of grain.

MODERATOR: We also made similar inquiries in Dašice.

Audio effects—teleprinter and fade

STUDIO ANNOUNCER 1: We have a telex from our colleague Pavel Kačer in Dašice.

STUDIO ANNOUNCER 2 (*reading telex*): We are constantly working on new improvements for the indicator. Eventually it will be used not only for harvesting, but also for sowing grain, for spreading fertilizer, and for adaptation to several other agricultural machines. We are also improving the sensor of the indicator so that the harvester operator will be forced to modify his running speed according to the reading of the indicator.

STUDIO ANNOUNCER 1: Our colleague in Dašice also sent this taped interview with Mr Jiří Pinkas, Chief of the Technical Department.

Tape

MR JIŘÍ PINKAS: We are producing indicators not only for the E–512 and the E–516 harvesters, but also for other kinds of threshing machines. We hope eventually to design indicators for any kind of agricultural machine available in the country.

MODERATOR: Well, that covers our field report on the grain loss indicator.

STUDIO ANNOUNCER 1: Yes, by keeping the running speed of the harvester within the optimum range on the dial, the operator will know that he is keeping grain loss to a minimum.

STUDIO ANNOUNCER 2: And the trials in the field have shown it to be an important device for farm co-operatives. Soon, different kinds of indicators will be designed for other agricultural machines as well.

MODERATOR: Now to round out our report on the grain loss indicator, we have a last comment from Stanislav Hudec, an economist with the Doubravice Agricultural Co-operative in Svitava.

Tape

MR STANISLAV HUDEC: The indicator is not a heavy investment. And I think every agricultural co-operative can afford to have such a device which keeps agricultural costs low and minimizes losses. Last year, with the indicator in full use, we had our highest grain yield in years.

MODERATOR (*Closing remarks*).

Audio effects—music bridge

Glenn Powell

Radio Noon:
farm broadcasting
in Canada

*In the past forty years, farm production has changed radically,
and so also has farm broadcasting. Crops are specialized, techniques are complicated, marketing is highly temperamental. And
mistakes are costly! Would-be farm broadcasters must know agriculture. It even helps to have a little manure on your boots.*

Farm radio within the Canadian Broadcasting Corporation (CBC) is essentially the sum of several regional
broadcasts. The size of the country—the second largest in
the world and stretching some 6,500 kilometres through five
time zones—makes it impossible to meet the daily information needs of all farmers with a single national broadcast.
The corporation's regional broadcast production centres,
linked through broadcast line facilities, telex and telephone, reflect the types of farming and the interests of
the rural communities within each specific region.

While the focus of this article will be on the English-
language radio service, CBC provides also a separate service for French-speaking farmers. This programme is

The author, Glenn Powell, is national agriculture reporter for the Canadian
Broadcasting Corporation's Radio News, Toronto, Canada.

broadcast primarily for the farmers in the province of Quebec and a few surrounding regions where there are also several French-speaking rural communities. The programme provides a brief summary of the major farm markets, but concentrates on news of particular interest to farmers. In addition to CBC farm broadcasters, free-lance correspondents provide regular contributions from points across Canada, the United States and Europe.

The environment plays an important part in establishing a format for any farm programme. The regional broadcasts must reflect the production of their region. For example, there is little sense in providing information for apple growers in an area that does not produce apples; or, devoting much air time to dairy policy when beef production is the major livestock operation of the region. The problem facing the Toronto-based production team is that just outside the big urban centre, there are practically all types of farming, except tropical crops and hard wheat. Not all types of farms are to be found in abundance, but the broadcast is heard on the vineyards and peach farms of the southern part of the province; livestock and poultry farms in the central part of the district; and the cash-crop farmers, whether they be involved in fruits, vegetables, corn (maize), soft wheat, or soybeans. There are also the very specialized units such as mink ranching, bee-keeping, and fish farming, none of which are large in number but combined add significantly to the farm economy of the region and to the complexity of the broadcast service.

Most of the region is gently rolling arable land with soil types varying from light sandy soil used for tobacco production, to heavy clay which is used for permanent pasture and hay. The broadcast signal also extends to the forest areas where lumbering becomes more important to the economy than farming.

The crop season is basically six months from April to September, with a frost-free period normally from mid-May to early September. Summer temperatures will range from 25º to 33º C, and winter temperatures will often be —10º to —20º C. The freezing temperatures and a constant snow cover, reaching perhaps 2 to 3 metres in some districts, make it necessary to provide housing and feed for livestock and poultry during the winter months from November to March. As a result, winter production costs on Canadian farms are significantly higher than during the rest of the year.

Because of the great variation in climate, soil, topography, farm production and marketing systems across the country, no less than eleven of CBC radio's production centres provide a regional, English-language, radio information service for farmers and rural residents. Each programme has its unique aspects: fishing in the coastal regions; the grain market in western Canada; markets, weather reports, and pesticide-control information in the fruit- and vegetable-producing area.

The programme chosen for this study is the one produced in Toronto, the capital city of the province of Ontario. This province is not only a major agricultural province but also the heart of Canada's industrial activity. Toronto and its suburbs have a population of about 3 million people. The broadcast signal of the 50-Kilowatt AM transmitter has a potential audience of about 5 million people.

While the target audience of the farm broadcast is the farmers in the area reached by the signal, the programme is also designed to provide information and maintain the interest of all listeners whether they be farmers or urban residents. The occupations, life-styles, and habits of the urban listeners show a wide variation and the same holds true for those on the farm.

As farm units have become more specialized, so too have the interests of the farmers and their requirements for information. Most farms are no longer the general production units they were twenty or thirty years ago. Poultry is perhaps the most specialized of the agricultural sector. The egg producer with a laying flock of 50,000 is not particularly interested in what is happening to the price of cattle, except for his concern about how much it is going to cost his family for a cut of beef at the supermarket; but the egg farmer is very interested in any change in the egg-marketing policy that will affect the profit picture of his farm unit. Both the egg producer and the beef farmer will be interested in the supply and price of grain that may change production costs in the months ahead. So while there are many specialized interests to be served in the broadcast, there are also common issues that must be given consideration. Consumers, of course, are concerned with any developments in the food production system that will affect the supply and price of food.

CBC has developed its farm programming in the midday period because this is the time of day when most farmers are at home for dinner, the main meal of the day. 'Pass the potatoes and turn up the farm broadcast' is often heard at table. The widespread use of portable transistor radios, radios on tractors, and perhaps even recording equipment in some farm offices has to some extent reduced the importance of the time of the broadcast, but the convenient common denominator is still the noon-hour time period.

Farmers naturally have less time to listen during the busy planting and harvesting seasons, but relatively more leisure to listen during the winter months. One experiment to spread the farm information over a longer period of the total two-hour programme met strong resistance from the farmers. In rather blunt terms, they informed CBC they simply did not have time to sit around waiting for the various segments of farm information that were interspersed with music, and other non-farm features. While this format appeared to be logical to the programme director, to the farmers it was not the radio service they were accustomed to, nor was it the service they wanted. The farmers won.

The radio station

CBC radio station in Toronto is but one of many operated by the corporation as part of a publicly owned national radio network to 'safeguard, enrich and strengthen the cultural, political, social and economic fabric of Canada'. Funds to operate the corporation are provided by the federal government in the form of an annual allocation approved by parliament. Additional revenue is obtained through commercial advertising on the corporation's television network; however, CBC radio has not had commercial advertising since 1972. It is worth mentioning that at the time advertising on the radio network was discontinued, the farm-consumer midday programme had the maximum commercials allowed under corporation policy.

Financing programme plans is, has, and probably always will be a problem. There never seems to be enough money to do all the things that a production team would like to do. The great distances to be covered in Canada make travel costs very expensive, and an additional allocation of funds could be well used to spend more time in the field. Improvements in equipment, buildings and facilities tend to come slowly. Priorities must be set and dealt with on a national basis. Often a crisis at one location becomes a matter of routine occurrence when compared with another location on the network. For the most part however, with proper planning and establishing priorities the farm broadcasters are able to provide the type and quality of programming expected of them.

The production unit

While overall CBC policy, programme scheduling and development is determined by senior management at the network level, the production team at each regional centre is under the administration of the local station manager. For day-to-day activities, the production team is responsible to the programme director. All members of the production team are employees of CBC, and while some members of the team are employed on a contract basis, the farm broadcasters are members of the corporation's permanent staff.

The production team for the two-hour time block consists of: one producer, one production assistant, two farm broadcasters, one consumer broadcaster, one announcer-host, one researcher, and one stenographer (part time).

The producer is ultimately responsible for the programme: direction and co-ordination of the team; accounting for the budget. The production assistant works directly with the producer and is responsible for selecting music, timing reports, arranging telephone calls for the broadcast and making the arrangements for guests to appear on the broadcast. Because of the specialized nature of their work, the agriculture broadcasters are self-assigning: selecting the stories, researching, writing, editing and presenting the report on-air. In addition to their major role on the noon-hour programme, the farm broadcasters also prepare and present a brief early morning report on farm news and markets, and a late-day summary of the livestock market prices. The consumer broadcaster prepares one or two reports per day on issues of interest to consumers. While the attention of the consumer commentator is focused on the food industry, the reports may and often do range from best buys at the grocery stores to problems with children's clothing, or the cost of financing credit-card purchases. The announcer-host is responsible for the on-air flow of programme. He opens the programme with a billboard of the items and features to be heard that day, introduces the commentators and other guests, and does the on-air linking of the programme segments. The research assistant gathers story ideas and facts necessary for in-depth treatment of reports and for replying to listeners' questions.

Each morning the entire unit meets to discuss plans for the broadcast that day. This meeting serves to co-ordinate the production team, often resulting in the consumer commentator and the farm broadcasters working on different aspects of the same story. In addition, the producer will hold regular meetings to discuss long-term plans, such as remote broadcasts, budgets, vacation schedules, etc.

Staff training has until recently been mostly on-the-job training. A start has been made to correct this inadequate situation with the development of a staff training unit as part of corporation policy. A first set of training courses was conducted for a period of one week, with each course having a total of four broadcasters from different regional production centres. The training was basically in writing and presentation for radio, and designed to help each participant recognize both his strengths and weaknesses. The course instructors were not specialists in agricultural broadcasting, but in drama, announcing and writing. They worked with the farm broadcasters to present material so that the programme would have more appeal to the general audience.

The Toronto production unit has office space located adjacent to the studio facilities which it uses for the two-hour broadcast period. The broadcast team also has access to the studio facilities for a one-hour period before the broadcast and a half-hour after the broadcast. These periods are used for recording interviews, and for mixing or editing as may be required.

The studio is equipped with a mono console, four microphones on a circular table for the broadcasters, with both a digital clock and sweep clock to facilitate back-timing while the programme is on the air. All microphones are equipped with talk-back switches to maintain liaison with the control room. The control room contains a mixing console, two turntables, three tape-record/playback machines, three cartridge playback machines, and telephone equipment capable of recording calls or taking calls live on-air. The telephone equipment enables conference calls of several speakers to be either recorded or put directly on-air.

Most on-location recordings are done on cassette. If editing is required, the cassette is first dubbed to tape. Both farm broadcasters have a cassette recorder, and have access to reel-to-reel recorders. In the office are two playback/editing machines and one turntable.

Information for the broadcast comes from many sources: news wire service, both Canadian and international; daily, weekly and monthly publications; CBC broadcasters, reports from other regions; government press releases and tape services; industry, press and public relations officials; telephone interviews; and freelance contributors. Perhaps the most important source of information is the broadcaster's own personal contact with farmers, government spokesmen and industry executives. The development of a successful broadcast depends directly on the depth of understanding of the subject and the contacts built over the years by the broadcast team. CBC's farm broadcasters are professional agriculturists and most were born and raised on a farm. They are familiar with farm problems, the food-production system and the rural way of life. As pointed out to one new arrival on the staff several years ago 'to join this team you have to have a little manure on your boots'. A check was quickly made of the young commentator's shoes. Fortunately, I had just returned from a trip to the stockyards and immediately passed the unofficial initiation established by my new colleagues.

The programme

For almost forty years rural programming has been an integral part of the radio schedule of CBC. In 1939, the first farm programme, fifteen minutes in length, was broadcast as an experiment. Such was its success that within three months the programme was expanded to thirty minutes. Listening to the daily noon-hour farm broadcast soon became a regular part of the lives of many farm families in Canada. Today, farm programming continues to occupy the midday time period of the CBC radio network, 12.00 to 14.00 hours, Monday to Friday. But just as the social and economic patterns of farming have changed dramatically over the years so have the emphasis and style of the farm broadcast.

Perhaps not surprisingly, farm broadcasting in Canada began mostly because of the demand and persistence of a farmer. About to take over the farm established by his father, a young farmer was deeply concerned that farmers did not have access to up-to-date market information and news that would affect their farm-management decisions. The farm publications provided a service but by the time printed material reached the farm, market prices and conditions had often changed. Several radio stations in the United States, some of which could be heard in Canada, and a few private (commercially operated) stations in Canada had begun a radio information service for farmers, but the then developing national radio system still had no farm programme. The young farmer presented his suggestion to the senior executives of what was later to become the Canadian Broadcasting Corporation.

The proposal for a farm programme was not immediately accepted but neither was the young farmer prepared to take 'no' for an answer. After several meetings, the persistence of the young farmer paid off. His request for a farm programme was granted and at the same time he was asked to establish the format for the farm broadcast. From this initial assignment he went on to establish farm broadcasts at the major radio production centres across Canada, each serving the particular needs of the farmers in the broadcast area.

The early farm broadcasts included market reports, news of special interest to farmers and a dramatized farm family serial. This serial adopted the short daily episode technique dealing with the 'real-life' happenings of a fictional farm family. The format proved highly successful, and in a little more than a year from the beginning of the first farm broadcast, similar programmes, each with its own farm family serial, were launched at the major regional radio production centres across Canada. Farm commentators were selected for each broadcast centre both for their ability to communicate and for their knowledge of agricultural production in the region. (In the coastal regions of the Atlantic provinces and British Columbia on the Pacific, the interests of fishermen were given special attention in fish broadcasts, and the administrative office to supervise the broadcasts became the Farms and Fisheries Department.)

The following is a sequence guide to a two-hour programme:

12.00 Announcer's introduction to Radio Noon national news, from the network newsroom.
12.14 Announcer's billboard of programme features.
Sports report.
Music.
12.20 Farm news highlights.
12.23 Farm market report.
12.30 Farm weather forecast.
12.31 Farm news, features and commentary.
12.40 Music.
12.42 Consumer report.
12.47 Music.
12.50 Feature item.
12.55 Interview with guest for the phone-in show.

13.00 National news.

13.10 Phone-in programme: listeners invited to phone with their questions for special guest of the day. Topic changes daily except Thursday, which is gardener's day with a horticulturist in the studio to answer questions.

14.00 Extro.

Recent years have seen many changes in the food-production industry. The number of farmers and fishermen as a percentage of the total population has declined dramatically. Production per farmer, however, has increased by more than 300 per cent in the last twenty-five years. The capital investment in farming has doubled in the past five years. It is estimated that one in every four Canadians is now employed somewhere in the food production, processing and distribution chain or in industries supplying machinery, fuel, fertilizer and other inputs for the food industry. This shift in economic and social patterns has had a marked impact on the style and emphasis of the farm broadcasts. In the past ten years, the farm broadcast has developed into a magazine-style programme maintaining the essential farm news and market information but becoming much broader in its choice and treatment of material to be included in the broadcast. This trend is not likely to alter in the future particularly as new and more sophisticated direct information services become available to farmers.

The objectives of the two-hour Radio Noon time period might be summarized as follows:

To provide essential information in a service programme which will interest and assist both the primary producer and the consumer.

To evaluate and interpret trends and developments which affect the primary producer and/or the consumer.

To provide an opportunity for public dialogue at all points in the food chain (production, distribution, marketing, pricing).

To provide information and commentary on municipal, provincial and federal government policies as they affect the people of the broadcast region and the nation.

To provide an informative, interesting and entertaining programme designed to gain and hold the attention of a growing general audience.

The Radio Noon programmes are heard in each region, Monday to Friday, 12.00 to 14.00 hours. They are preceded by a three-hour general interest magazine-type programme that is produced by the network centre and broadcast on a time-delay basis so that it is heard from 09.00 to 12.00 hours local time throughout the five time zones. Immediately following the Radio Noon programmes is a school broadcast or music programme depending on the period of the year.

The opening of the programme is ad libbed to promote the general easy listening style of the programme. Some locations do have a theme song to identify the broadcast but most production units discarded theme songs and standard introductions several years ago.

Budget limitations prohibit extensive use of field workers or stringers, though government market reporters provide a daily information service to the broadcast. Some market intelligence is also received on a regular basis from the information officers of the farm commodity organizations. The government reporter at the livestock market is provided with a microphone with broadcast link. Routine commodity reports are prepared on a mimeographed form for easy reading and quick analysis. Telephone reports are accepted from other market offices. At some broadcast production centres, the farm programme is assisted by occasional reports from editors of the rural weekly newspapers. And in some cases, farmers who are able to write and voice reports are regular contributors.

Located in the large metropolitan city of Toronto, the farm broadcast team often finds it difficult to maintain personal contact with the farm audience. Traffic problems that seem to be part of every city and the distance to the major farm areas are significant factors in determining the field visits a broadcaster can make to gather information and record interviews. In effect, the city location of the radio production centre limits personal contact with the audience. On the other hand there are some advantages. The city is the provincial capital and centre of government and commercial activity. The broadcasters have access to government officials, industry and agricultural business executives, wholesale produce and livestock markets, and leaders of the farm organizations and producer marketing boards.

Field trips are usually undertaken for a full day, perhaps two or three days, by one member of the team. While in the field the broadcaster will report to the broadcast by telephone, but if the occasion warrants it, broadcast line facilities will be arranged. Within the limitations of budget and time, an attempt is made to have one of the farm broadcasters in the field as often as possible. Reports from 'remote locations' not only give information to all listeners but also serve to alert the listeners in an area that one of the broadcast team is in the region. This often results in a listener making a special effort to contact the broadcaster with a tip to a story from that area.

For major annual events such as the International Plowing Match, the Farm Machinery Show, and the Royal Agricultural Winter Fair, the entire programme will be done on-location using mobile broadcast facilities. Broadcasting from these events inevitably produces special problems that require instant solutions: 'live guests' fail to arrive in time for the broadcast, a power failure knocks out the equipment, a gust of wind sweeps away the broadcasters script, or only minutes before air time the technician discovers the broadcast line between the location and master control is not functioning. On-location broadcasting is a test in coping with the unexpected, but it does enable the broadcast team to meet a large cross-section of the listeners.

Contests offer another technique to assist in developing a rapport with the listeners: 'In twenty-five words or less describe what the agricultural industry means to you.' The author of the winning entry received a garden tractor. 'Guess the amount of milk a cow will give at a special dairy-day programme.' The entire broadcast was done on-location on this day, featuring all aspects of the dairy industry. The cow was milked during the broadcast and the winner of the contest won a year's supply of dairy products for his family. At another production centre the farm broadcasters held a 'name the steer contest'. They purchased a steer and followed its progress in the feedlot. Regular interviews were done with the farmer feeding the steer. Records were kept of the costs of feed and any medication. Stories were done on the marketing and processing of the meat. In this way the broadcasters were able to provide the listeners, over an extended period, with an intimate story of beef production. The winning entry in the contest was treated to dinner at a fine restaurant. The farm broadcasters reported that the profit from feeding the steer failed to match the expense of a night on the town!

In an effort to meet the programme objectives, and in addition to fulfilling other daily programme commitments, the production unit regularly undertakes special projects to promote more understanding between the rural and urban sectors of the society.

The broadcast team organized an 'agriculture day' at which all of the farm commodity marketing boards and organizations were invited to take part and tell their story to the public. Each farm group set up a small booth to explain their product and how it reached the consumer. Small samples of many food products were given to the public; in fact, by visiting all the booths a visitor could obtain a complete lunch. More than twenty farm groups participated in the day and it provided ample opportunity for both the farm commentators and the consumer commentator to interview the producers.

At another broadcast location, successful 'mobile' farm broadcasts have been developed. Listeners were invited to join a tour of farms in the region. By following the tour and listening to their car radios, they were not only able to see what was happening on the farm but also to hear the interview of the farmer describing his operation. Remote mobile equipment is used to broadcast the signal back to the base station and transmitter. To reduce the vehicle traffic and keep the programme on time, buses were used to transport many of the listeners who wished to make the tour.

Another broadcast team, faced with covering a full-scale investigation into the future of the railways in western Canada, decided that the only way to do the job was to attend virtually all the commission's hearings. It turned out there were more than a hundred meetings but, by making use of the farm broadcasters in the adjoining region, they were able to keep an almost daily check of the progress of the investigation. When the commission made its report public, a one-hour special programme for the entire region was broadcast by the farm commentators who had followed the commission in and out of all the locations during the year of hearings. It was an issue that touched all of the people as the report of the commission, if implemented, would have a large part to play in the transportation network of the future.

Evaluation

Programme evaluation is essential to: improving the planning system, providing management with information needed to make decisions about programmes, and providing producers and production personnel with information to help them improve the broadcast. The evaluation report should provide a measurement of how effectively a programme is achieving its purpose and objectives.

While regular evaluation of the farm broadcast is not carried out as part of CBC policy, periodic evaluations are made. A three-member evaluation team is selected from senior production and/or management personnel within the corporation, with at least one member from a region other than the region in which the broadcast is heard. On occasion, a member of the evaluation team will be an individual from outside the corporation but one who has a broad background in communications. The evaluation committee is expected not only to listen to the programme but also to solicit comments and opinions from the production team, local station management and listeners. The evaluation team is expected to file a report commenting on the content, production, talent, overall evaluation and suggestions for improvement.

An audience survey is another means of evaluation, and CBC has conducted extensive surveys of the farm broadcast in some regions, but not all. For the Toronto region noon-time period, a questionnaire was mailed to a random selection of farm and non-farm residences. From the survey, it was learned that the majority of listeners were not farmers. This was not surprising as the number of farmers is only a small percentage of the total population, but it was revealing to learn that as much as 83 per cent of the listeners were not farmers. Of the farmers who did listen to the programme more than half listened all the time, and of the non-farmers almost half reported listening to the broadcast five days a week. It was also learned that approximately half of all farmers in the region listened to the farm broadcast at least one day of the week, and that the majority of farm listeners were from the larger farms with gross incomes higher than the regional average. The survey also determined listener interest in various segments of the broadcast. In summary, the survey showed that not only did the broadcast have a substantial percentage of the farmers in the region listening on a regular, if not daily, basis but also there is a much larger number of non-farmers listening. It was from this information that a decision was made to emphasize all aspects of the food production system and as much as possible interpret the farm news for the non-farm audience.

For CBC, audience size is but one measure of a programme's success. It is an indication of listener acceptance to the programme schedule and to the specific programmes within that schedule. For certain programmes known to be of interest primarily to a minority audience, the corporation accepts the fact that the size of the audience will not compare favourably with competing stations which are programming mostly popular music and sports events. None the less, it is the objective of every production team to increase the size of its audience, and the farm broadcast is no exception.

Feedback to the programme also comes via listeners' letters and telephone calls requesting more information about a particular item heard on the broadcast. Requests for tapes or transcripts are discouraged although listeners are invited to come to the CBC offices to listen to an aircheck of the programme if they so wish. Sometimes a listener may not like or agree with an item that has been broadcast. If the criticism is justified and 'in good taste', the individual is given the opportunity to reply on a subsequent broadcast. Legal action has seldom resulted from statements made on the farm broadcast.

Special meetings have been held with groups of farmers to discuss the farm radio programme. A one-day session with twelve to fifteen farmers representing various areas and interests has proved most beneficial in establishing programme priorities. Also, meetings with the major farm organizations have led to ideas for specific programmes and changes in the general format of the broadcast. For example, with the development of farm-marketing boards (many of which have the authority to control production and establish the price to the producer), it has become less important to provide the daily market price of many commodities. However, it has become more important to provide farmers with more information about long-range forecasts, trends and trade prospects. It has also become a regular part of the farm broadcasters' task to inform both farmers and consumers of the activities and decisions of the various marketing boards.

Plans are now being developed to establish programme advisory councils for the regional farm radio broadcasts. The advisory councils, representing various segments of the audience—both farmers and consumers—will meet regularly with CBC management and the local production team to discuss the programme. It is hoped that the advisory council system will provide regular, meaningful dialogue between the broadcasters and the audience.

Perhaps the most effective feedback system has developed from the farm broadcasters' regular contact with the farm organizations and the farm audience. Attending meetings and travelling in the region provide excellent opportunities for the broadcasters to gather opinion and comment on the programme.

If the long-term objective of CBC's farm radio service can be summarized by stating that the programmes are to provide information and entertainment for the farm audience while keeping in mind the interests of the general audience, then it can be said that the programme is meeting that objective. To place a qualitative or quantitative measure of success is difficult, if not impossible. As an experienced broadcaster once said: 'There are no absolutes in broadcasting . . . there is always room for improvement . . . you are only as good as your last broadcast.'

While many farmers over the years have related occasions where the broadcast has helped them achieve a better price for their produce, there is at least one example in which the broadcast had a part to play in saving the life of an infant. A phone call was received just before air time from a doctor in the children's ward of a large city hospital requesting assistance. An infant was unable to digest cow's milk and other commercial baby formulas. Almost in desperation, the doctor wanted to try to feed goat's milk to the child but had no idea where to obtain a supply. The story was broadcast on the farm programme and within a matter of minutes the hospital received calls from no less than six goat breeders offering to supply milk for the baby. Within a few days the child was on the way to recovery.

Observations

During almost forty years of farm broadcasting in Canada, both the farm and the broadcasting situations have changed. Agriculture has developed from the former general-purpose multi-crop farms to high-volume one-crop industries. The number of farmers has significantly decreased, but the overall population—all of whom are directly affected by farming, marketing, and prices—has increased. The entire agricultural-industrial complex has become more complicated and compartmentalized: feeds, fertilizer, production of mechanized and electronic farm implements, inspection storage, transport, marketing, distribution, pricing, consumer reactions. Farming is also affected by national policies, world trade, and events in other parts of the world.

Similarly, broadcasting styles have changed from the original programmes stressing general techniques and farm forums for self-help to magazine-style programmes touching on topics of interest to the general audience: news and weather, farm fairs, prices, commodity indexes, new techniques and machines, and government infrastructure programmes. This is especially so, as farmers gain access to other sources of technical information. More recently, the formats have switched to investigative reports and analysis, and in this area much more will be done in the future.

In farm broadcasting, it is essential that the reporters and producers know farming—both scientifically and from practical experience. This is no less essential for a developed country like Canada, than it would be for developing countries that still use the majority of their manpower resources for agriculture.

Finally, an important and often overlooked aspect of rural programming is training. Few farmers are ready to go on mike. Few broadcasters have ever been farmers. It is necessary to bridge these two disciplines, provide the personnel and facilities for training, experiment with new formats, techniques and approaches, especially in the production of depth studies, backgrounders, investigative reports and analysis. Either within the broadcasting organization or the production unit, there must be provision for regular in-service training, or the opportunity to participate in workshops and seminars, in order to continually update knowledge and techniques.

[B.10] CC. 78/XXVI-5/A